TORONTO REGION

The Family-Tested Guide to

SUMMER FUN

The most useful digest of
Torontonians' favourite
family attractions

Word
— of —
Mouth
Production

Word-of-Mouth Production
299 Booth Avenue
Toronto, Ontario M4M 2M7, Canada
Tel.: (416) 462-0670
Fax: (416) 462-0682
funplace@istar.ca
home.istar.ca/~funplace

Writing and photos: **Nathalie Prézeau**
Design and Layout: **Publisher Friendly** (416) 980-0774
Illustrations: **Johanne Pepin** (450) 456-3980
Printing: **AGMV Marquis** (514) 954-1131
Translation: **Julie Bonin** (514) 852-4264, **Célyne Gagnon** (250) 752-8798
Corporate Relations: **Debbie Ackers**
Proofreading: **Kerstin McCutcheon, Julie Sabourin**

Canadian Cataloguing in Publication Data

Prézeau, Nathalie, 1960 –
Toronto region: the family-tested guide to summer fun:
the most useful digest of Torontonians' favourite family attractions

Includes index
ISBN 0-9684432-1-4

1. Family recreation – Ontario – Toronto Region – Guidebooks.
2. Toronto Region (Ont.) – Guidebooks. I. Title.

FC3097.18.P743 2000   917.13'541044   C00-900283-9
F1059.5.T683P743 2000

A word from the author

When visiting a new city, nothing compares to having friends living there who can guide us to their favourite attractions. Word-of-mouth is gold for the simple pleasure of passing on the knowledge of a great outing and the enjoyment of its long lasting memories.

Allow me to be just that for you. It took my family four summers to visit the sites listed in this guide. Here, you will find personal descriptions, tips, humorous narration, comprehensive information boxes and my best snap-shots of these places. Most importantly, this guide will help you make the most of popular attractions, while also taking you off-the-beaten track and focusing on activities interesting to children 12 years and under.

When selecting summer attractions for this digest from my year-round guide *Toronto: The Family-tested Guide to Fun Places*, I chose to leave out any outings not suitable for families staying in a hotel. For example, trout and fruit picking farms were not included and many activities were left out in favour of similar ones more conveniently located close to downtown Toronto.

Take a moment to read the inside cover on "How to use this guide" and get yourself a map of the Greater Toronto Area. It is the best way to make *Summer Fun* work for you.

I sincerely hope this guide will contribute to an outstanding summer exploration of Toronto with your loved ones.

Have fun!

Nathalie Prézeau
(with great help from François, Laurent and Roxane)

This book is dedicated to my godmother Gisèle Lavigne.
Everywhere she went was a fun place to be!

TABLE OF CONTENTS

We would love to hear from you!
You may send us your comments, suggestions or outing stories to:

Word-of-Mouth Production
299 Booth Avenue
Toronto, ON, Canada
M4M 2M7
Tel.: (416) 462-0670
Fax: (416) 462-0682
E-Mail: funplace@istar.ca

♥ Ontario Place

Best affordable mix of activities
for all ages, right on Lake Ontario;
rides, Children's Village playground,
water park, pedal boat and canoe rentals,
Imax movies, naval museum...
(see page 10)

AMUSEMENT PARKS

PLAYDIUM TORONTO

Rumble in the jungle

At the crossroads of John and Richmond Streets, a huge multi-screen cube dominates with darting images to lure you to the Paramount cinema. A little farther, the Playdium Toronto awaits you with its frantic world

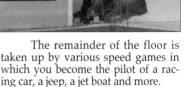

of perpetually moving lights, mezzanines overlooking a red climbing wall and four floors of sheer dizzying and ear-splitting excitement. We're in the heart of downtown Toronto's most animated neighbourhood.

The first attraction that catches my pre-preadolescent's eye is a virtual rollercoaster, set in a two-person cabin which rotates in all directions. Soon however, he is distracted by the Brave Fire Fighters display. This is a great substitute for the myriads of "shoot the enemy" games. Here, the enemy is fire and the weapon a hose, with which he shoots a virtual stream against the roaring blaze displayed on the large screen. It proves highly entertaining.

The first level also features a small area with a few games of skill for younger children, but these pale against the 300 surrounding attractions.

The remainder of the floor is taken up by various speed games in which you become the pilot of a racing car, a jeep, a jet boat and more.

On the second floor, older participants will head for the **Combat Zone** and **Target Zone** and their avalanche of hair-raising games (parent's nightmare!).

Make sure not to miss Combatica, the most original attraction in this area. Here, you can attend or participate in combat by way of new technology that transposes real fighters' jumps and kicks taking place on the floor of a special ring, onto virtual adversaries on the screen.

Our favourite section however was the **Sport Zone** on the third floor where you'll engage in truly physically interactive games. You can toss some in the Basketball and Football games or kick one off in Soccer. Strong ones can even cast a line to enormous Fish (outfitted with deep-sea fishing equipment!).

We also had a blast rafting down all sorts of rivers. Side by side and facing the large screen, we madly paddled to avoid being engulfed in a giant whirlpool or eaten by a huge Tyrannosaurus. We giggled and sweated tons with each descent!

Elsewhere, my young dare-devil crashed at liberty on his virtual snow-board, without a scratch, while I skied down expert runs. We played long and hard at table hockey; sending the puck sliding back and forth atop a cushion of air.

Then, it was off to my son's first sky-diving jump! Strapped into his harness, goggles in place and hands on the handles, he "jumped" the virtual plane, taking in the panoramic views as he manoeuvred around. The hang-glider ride left nothing to be desired either!

TIPS (fun for 6 years +)
• There are two ways to play. With Value Play, you put any cash value you want on your Play Card. On my first visit to the Playdium, it took me less than 15 minutes to squander my $10 credit! If you lack practice with electronic games, you'll quickly get eliminated. Don't hesitate to ask the many attendants how the games work. With Time Play, you pay a fixed amount for one or two hours of unlimited access to the games. You may ask an attendant to "freeze" the time on your card to rest, have a snack (or to take the kids to the washroom!).
• It is possible to block access to violent games on the magnetic card you buy for your child.

Amidst all of this excitement, Toronto Playdium offers a unique attraction: **The Playdium City Diner**, with its great children's meal selection for $5 and less. You will find tables and comfortable seats overlooking climbers ascending the red wall and the many patrons enjoying the adjacent mezzanines. Each table comes equipped with a large screen and four levers to play video games. When we visited, we saw video clips of city landscapes, running in slow and fast motion. Soon, you will be able to order from the screen, visit an art gallery, play games or watch clips while you wait for your meal…free of charge!

INFORMATION	Downtown
Playdium Toronto	**Toronto**
(416) 260-1400	**5-min.**
www.playdium.com	

 Schedule: Open year-round, from 11 am to 11 pm (closes at 2 am Thursday to Saturday).

 Admission: On a pay-as-you-play basis debited from your Playdium Play Card (ranges from 50¢ to $5 per game) or $17.95 for 1-hour of unlimited play.

Directions: 126 John Street (between Adelaide and Richmond, south of Queen Street), Toronto.

NEARBY ATTRACTIONS

ONTARIO PLACE

In the first place

Ontario Place is an excellent water park as well as a perfect playground. The numerous rides offer adrenalin rushes for young and old. It is at times educational, with science shows and the Haida Naval Museum. It is entertaining with Imax movies and numerous musical shows. Finally, it is a conservation area, with pedal boats, canoes and gigantic green spaces. Whenever we are looking for fun attractions, we should always consider Ontario Place in the first place!

The **Children's Village**, located on the east side of Ontario Place is covered with a big coloured canopy protecting visitors from rain or sun. It's a superb, gigantic playground offering activities for children 12 years and under.

The area designed for toddlers offers a pen full of coloured balls, an inflated mattress to jump on, tunnels, a playhouse, swings and many more activities to discover. For older kids, there's a foam forest, an enormous inflated mattress, a gigantic slide, alleys to explore as well as a myriad of climbing structures.

Ontario Place's architecture is an attraction in itself. Children enjoy watching people from the bridges linking the huge white pods built atop the water. The Imax theatre is attached to the white structure.

Don't miss the **Japanese Temple Bell** which children can ring themselves. It is located close to the pedal boat area.

With the Play All Day Pass, visitors are allowed on the rides. Younger children will gain access to the Mini Bumper Boats (3 years+, 49" max.), while the older ones will want to ride on the bigger boats (48"+).

Those who reach the foot pedals will have access to the Whiz Kids' battery-powered go-karts (4 years+). Expect a long line-up. During our last visit, the dads waited in line for a jet boat ride while we stuffed ourselves with Beaver Tails, a treat sold on the premises, as we waited in line for go-karts.

The Play-All-Day Pass allows everybody to play on the 9-hole Mini Green or use the pedal boats. It allows anyone willing to sit for half an hour to watch an Imax movie at the **Cinesphere** (this is somewhat hard on young eardrums), or to attend the new attraction **Grossology: The Impolite Science of the Human Body**.

The Wilderness Adventure Ride (42"+) is a raft ride through canyons that features animated characters. I was worried that the final 40-foot drop would be too challenging, but my little one wanted more! In fact, the descent went slower than I imagined. With his raincoat on, our young adventurer came out almost dry. I can't say the same thing about his father!

The Megamaze is a multi-level labyrinth. It consists of seven mazes with optical illusions, puzzling for younger children. The Mars Simulator Ride (36"+) mimics a space shuttle on a mission. Moving seats and big screen help create a fascinating effect.

TIPS (fun for 2 years +)

• Ground admission is the cheapest way to visit. This option may be interesting if you visit with children 5 years and under. It will allow you to play in the **Children's Village** and to watch the outdoor children's shows at the Festival Stage and the Island Stage.

• The **Legoland** attraction has unfortunately been cancelled!... What a shame!

• You may upgrade your ground admission to a Play-All-Day Pass, giving you access to the rides and water park, at two booths on the site.

• A footbridge connects the western tip of Ontario Place to the site's West exit on the shore. It's a good shortcut back to the parking lot on the west end side after an exhausting day.

• If you go on the Wilderness Adventure Ride, visit the Autoclic table. You'll want to see your picture, taken as you're coming down the flume. Bring a raincoat or garbage bag to cover yourself if you want to stay dry.

• The **Benson & Hedges Symphony of Fire** and the **Canadian International Air Show** are held at Ontario Place each summer. They are free with ground admission to Ontario Place (reserved seating is available for an extra fee). Call to find out the exact dates.

• Finish your day by exploring the HMCS Haida Naval Museum, a huge gray warship parked by Ontario Place. Admission is included with the Play-All-Day Pass. More on page 63.

• More on Ontario Place water park on page 122.

NEARBY ATTRACTIONS
Harbourfront Centre (10-min.).... p. 38
Historic Fort York (5-min.).......... p. 110

INFORMATION	Downtown
Ontario Place	Toronto
(416) 314-9900	10-min.
www.ontarioplace.com	

Schedule: Open daily from Victoria Day to Labour Day (closed during the 4 days following Victoria Day), from 10 am. Closes at 6 pm in May and weekdays in June until mid-June. Closes at midnight the rest of the season.

Admission: Ground admission is $10/6 years and over. Play All Day Pass (including the ground admission plus access to all the rides and water games) is $24.50/106 cm (42 inches)+ up to 54 years, $11/4 years up to 106 cm (42 inches), $15/55 years and over. FREE for children 3 and under.

Other costs: $9 for parking on the site ($12 to $15 on event days).

Directions: 955 Lake Shore Blvd., Toronto. Located on Toronto's waterfront between Strachan Avenue and Dufferin Street.

CENTREVILLE /TORONTO ISLANDS

Islanders for a day

Did you know that an amusement park existed in 1800 at the very same place today's Toronto Island Airport sits? In 1909, a baseball stadium was added to this park. Did you know that it's in this very stadium that Babe Ruth hit his first professional home run?

The **Toronto Islands** might have lost their identity as centres of recreation after the 1930's when the stadium was closed, the amusement park demolished and the air-

port constructed, but they have since reclaimed the title with a vengeance, with over 1.2 million visitors every year.

Ferry ride

The adventure starts before you even reach the Islands with a ferry ride, the only way to reach them.

My little sailor was tickled pink, unsure whether to check the panoramic view of the CN Tower and the tall buildings close to it, look at planes taking off from the Toronto Island Airport, gaze at the white sailboats manoeuvring on Lake Ontario, or to simply explore the many bridges on the ferry itself.

Three ferry boats service the Islands. The ferry that reaches **Centre Island** brings you closest to the **Centreville Amusement Park** and the bicycle rentals. It is the most popular, crossing every 15 minutes on weekends (for most of the day). The **Hanlan's Point** ferry services the western end of **Toronto Islands**, while **Ward's Island** ferry reaches the

eastern point. These two ferries cross every half-hour throughout the day.

Hanlan's Point

The **Hanlan's Point** ferry reaches the western end of the Islands. The amusement park is located approximately 3.5 km further so I don't recommend you take on the walk with young children, on a hot sunny day.

This part of the Islands includes the Toronto Island Airport, illuminated tennis courts, 2 wading pools, a trout pond and 2 beaches including the superb **Hanlan Beach**.

Ward's Island

The eastern part of the Islands is where the year-round residents live. Within a short walk from the dock, you can reach the boardwalk and the intimate **Ward's Beach**, interesting for its proximity to the boardwalk. It is almost impossible to resist a nosy peek as you stroll by the little postcard cottages close to this boardwalk. This is not the only temptation here as one of us is always sent on a mission to fetch good coffees at the tea room by the boardwalk.

Centre Island

Apart from the unavoidable **Centreville Amusement Park**, **Centre Island** also has a bike rental service offering tandem and 4-seaters, available to ride the 20km trail that criss-crosses the Islands.

Centreville Amusement Park

Centreville has the charm of a turn-of-the-century village. It is a small-scale amusement park. With its 24 small rides, Centreville is perfect for young families!

Our small group really loved the beautiful carousel, a feast for the eyes! It includes ostriches, zebras, lions, pigs, cats, giraffes as well as the traditional horses. The animals are laid out in three rows and turn rapidly as they go up and down to the sound of lively music. The little ones are fascinated by the train that rides through a long tunnel, by the

TIPS (fun for 2 years +)

• Don't forget the kids bathing suits so they can take advantage of the wading pools and/or the beaches.
• The waters along the south shore of the Islands are the cleanest waters in the area. The Islands act as a filter and their beaches are the farthest away from the sources of pollution. Environment Canada says we should not swim up to two days after a rain storm.
• Most people eat in the park outside **Centreville Amusement Park**'s walls. It has picnic tables, a playground and... numerous geese.
• The Centre Island ferry won't allow bikes aboard on summer weekends but the other two ferries always welcome them.
• More on our favourite swimming hole Hanlan's Beach on page 123.

NEARBY ATTRACTIONS
From Toronto Islands Ferry:
Harbourfront Centre (5-min.)........ p. 38
The Pier (10-min. walk)............... p. 75

antique cars set on tracks which they drive "themselves" and by the Swan Ride on the pond.

They're also pretty excited by the Bumble Bee Ride at the entrance. Older children appreciate the bumper boats and cars, the Lake Monster Coaster and the train through the Haunted Barrel ride. Those who like heights will want to try the Sky Ride cable-car or the Ferris wheel. Don't hesitate to try the Saugeen Lumber Co. Log Flume Ride, even with the smaller kamikazes. A small farm and a lovely wading pool are found on site.

INFORMATION	Downtown
City of Toronto (416) 392-8186 Islands Ferry Terminal (416) 392-8193	Toronto Islands

 Schedule: During the summer, the 3 ferries operate from 8 am until 11:45 pm. Schedules vary on weekdays.
Admission: Return fare is $5/adults, $2/students & seniors, $1/2-14 years, FREE for children less than 2 years old.
Directions: The Toronto Islands Ferry Terminal is located on Queen's Quay West, east of Bay Street. No cars allowed on the ferry.

Centreville Amusement Park (416) 203-0405
Schedule: Open daily Victoria Day until Labour Day and weekends during first 3 weeks in May and last 4 weeks in September, weather permitting. Opens from 10:30 am to 8 pm during July and August; closes between 5 pm and 7 pm the rest of the season.
Admission: (taxes not included) The All Day Ride Pass is $13.04 for visitors 4 feet tall and under and $18.65 for the others (plus taxes). Tickets for each ride can be bought individually.
Directions: Acessible by ferry, then a 10-min. walk from Centre Island docks.

CANADA'S WONDERLAND

Do your little ones measure up?

Very soon, we'll have to face a new reality. Our young kamikaze has just reached the 48-inch mark. This year, he'll be allowed into the big rides. His father and I will draw straws. The loser will have to ride with him in a gravity-defying attraction...

The height of children in your party is the most important factor to consider when planning your outing. I saw several children crying their hearts out after a long wait for a ride, as they were finding out (at the same time as their parents) that they had to turn back. Consult the table containing the required height for each ride, available at the park entrance.

Children measuring less than 40 inches tall have access to eighteen small rides, several shows, a large playground and the big water park.

When they pass the 40-inch mark, the new "big kids" can go on about 10 additional rides (about half the park's rides). But are they ready for the big thrills awaiting them? Free falls, speed, darkness and surprises? You be the judge. To help you out, there are Fun & Safety Guides, including a ride description, posted at each ride's entrance.

When children reach 44 inches tall, two-thirds of the rides become accessible to them. As soon as the children are 48 inches tall, they're allowed on most of Wonderland's 60 rides.

A good start

A line-up is a parent's worst nightmare. That's why I think there's only one way to make the experience enjoyable: arrive at opening time and go straight to your favourite kind of ride! Our first choice is the Thunder Run, going through the mountain (40"+). It puts you in good spirits for the day! Further on, you're sure to get wet (if you haven't covered yourself with a garbage bag) at the White Water Canyon and the Timberwolf Falls (both 40" +)!

Then, spend some time at the Candy Factory, a great playground where kids can use up lots of energy while you study the schedule of shows (included in the Wonderland map) to better plan your day.

Children's rides

Near the Candy Factory are two areas for children 8 years and under which include 22 rides altogether. If your children are comfortable with the Taxi Jam roller coaster in **Kidzville** (probably too much for children 3 years and under) you might want them to try the Ghoster Coaster (40"+) in **Hanna-Barbera Land**.

Our other favourite rides include the Frequent Flyers' Parachutes, the turning cups of the Flavourator, the big colourful maze by the Candy Factory, the Boulder Bumpers (bumper cars for all who dare) and the Hot Rock Raceway (slow racing cars for everyone) in **Hanna-Barbera Land**. Most of the other rides in **Kidzville** and **Hanna-Barbera Land** are pretty tame and don't last long enough for our liking, especially after waiting in line for a while.

In the **Medieval** section is the Speed City Raceway (cars run by 9-horsepower engines), for passengers 40 inches and over.

In the **World Exposition of 1890** section, there is the large antique carousel (36"+), the Great Whale of China (40"+) and the hilarious Watersnakes slides (40"+). Beware of that one too, you will definitely get wet! On the way out, young and old watch with fascination the "crazies" who leap from the top of the Xtreme Sky Flyer tower, a show in itself!

Mighty Canadian Minebuster (48"+) roller coaster and those (of horror, I suspect) of the Sky Rider passengers, tracing loops with their feet hanging in the air. For roller coaster fans, there's also the Vortex, the Dragon's Fyre, the Bat (all for 48"+) and the Top Gun (54"+). There's another series of rides meant to make anyone dizzy. A few are accessible to children of 44 inches or more.

Children's shows

The Playhouse Theatre in **Kidzville** runs an excellent little musical show several times a day. The theatre is covered and provides welcome shade in the midst of summer. If you want another break from the summer sun, your best option is to watch the sea lion show at Bedrock Aquarium, in **Hanna-Barbera Land**. Not only is the show interactive and entertaining, but the pool's cool water refreshes the whole area under the roof.

About the big rides

From **Splash Works**, we can hear the cries (of hysteria, I presume) of thrill-seekers riding at full speed on the

... and more

Live musical shows are featured on various interior and exterior stages. Aquatic shows are available at Arthur's Baye and professionals dive daily from atop the mountain waterfall.

Furthermore, there's the Paramount Action FX Theatre (44"+), a motion simulator with seats that move in sync with the action on the screen, fireworks shows and many other one-time events. Need anything else with that?

TIPS (fun for 3 years +)
• Canada's Wonderland has everything to please children of all ages but for children measuring 40 inches or less, I recommend Ontario Place's huge playground and water games or Centreville's rides (check pages 10, 12 & 122).
• Bring garbage bags to cover yourself on rides involving water.
• There is the Deluxe-Twelve option including 12 tickets for those who just intend to get on a few rides with the children or to have access to the Water Works.
• More on Wonderland's **Splash Works** section on page 136.

NEARBY ATTRACTION
McMichael Canadian Art (10-min.) p. 84

INFORMATION	**North**
Paramount Canada's **Wonderland** **• Vaughan** **(905) 832-7000** www.canadaswonderland.com	of Toronto 40-min.

 Schedule: Open during the weekends starting the first Sunday in May right through to Canadian Thanksgiving weekend and daily from Victoria Day to Labour Day. Open from 10 am to 10 pm minimum (closing times vary).

Admission: (taxes not included) $43/7 to 59 years or 48 inches+ tall, $21.50/3 to 6 years and seniors, FREE for children 2 years and under. Grounds admission only is $23. Parking is $6.50.

Directions: 9580 Jane Street, Vaughan. From Hwy 401, go north on Hwy 400, take exit 33 (Rutherford Road) near Vaughan if you're coming from the South or exit 35 (Major Mackenzie Dr.) if you're coming from the North.

❤ Kortright Waterfowl Park

Kortright's sanctuary houses over 90 different species. Free-roaming birds of all sizes, colours and calls greet you in a joyous cacophony in order to get your attention... and a few grains.

(see page 29)

ANIMALS
& FARMS

RIVERDALE FARM

Fieldmouse in the city

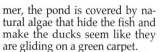

At Riverdale Farm, there are cows of all types, goats, sheep and large pigs. There are hens, roosters, chickadees, and large turkeys. All this in the heart of the city!

Personally, what brings me back to Riverdale Farm is its turn-of-the-century atmosphere and the beautiful flowery and softly steeped setting.

A path brings us to a lower level and a natural pond, our favourite spot. There, a small house sits with wire-mesh covered windows, in which kids like to imagine they're in a prison. During the sum-mer, the pond is covered by na-tural algae that hide the fish and make the ducks seem like they are gliding on a green carpet.

The cattle paddock by the farm's entrance, with its huge hairy cows, welcomes visitors.

On the other side of the gates, the horse paddock and the **Francey Barn** await you. That's where you might get a chance to see demonstrations such as ice cream making, horse groo-ming, and cow or goat milking. In the barn you'll find sheep, goats and don-keys. In late spring, you might have the chance to glimpse a cute new-born.

There's also the pig and poultry barn and further down, another pond beau-tifully surrounded by flowers. Make sure you drop by the **Meeting House** right in front. It offers children a play area with miniature farm animals and machines, and even craft material for a make-and-take activity from time to time.

Sometimes, you can catch a free horse-drawn ride around the site.

TIPS (fun for 2 years +)
• Call the farm to find out more about March Break, Easter, Christmas and Hal-loween special activities.
• Every September, on the weekend after Labour Day, there's great fun to be had at Riverdale Farm during the **Fall Festival**. Parliament Street is closed for the occasion. Families come in hordes to enjoy the Saturday morning pancake and sausage breakfast at the farm, browse through the merchandise of the many artisans installed for the weekend at the park bordering the farm, or to par-ticipate in the various activities sche-duled.

NEARBY ATTRACTION
Allan Gardens (5-min.).................. p. 90

INFORMATION Riverdale Farm (416) 392-6794	Downtown Toronto 15-min.

 Schedule: Open year-round from 9 am to 4 pm.
Admission: FREE
Directions: 201 Winchester St., Toronto. Take Parliament St., go north of Carlton Street, turn eastbound on Winchester.

TORONTO ZOO

Kid-friendly all year long

Sometimes, we adults tackle an itinerary through the zoo as if it were a shopping list. We just have to see all 5000 animals between lunch and naptime. Orangutan? Been there! Giraffes? Done that! Hippo?... "Darn! We missed the hippo!" And while we stand there, confounded in the midst of such a tragedy, we miss the sounds of our young explorers laughing in front of a small otter's cage.

It would take more than eight hours to tour all the trails shown on the Zoo's map. It is impossible to see it all in one day with children. Why not just relax and enjoy the visit at the children's pace?

The Zoo fascinates each child in a different way; most likely depending on the last books or videos that have struck their imagination. Therefore, it seems logical to adapt the visit according to their interest of the moment. The Visitor's Guide handed out at the admission gate is packed with useful information and includes a map, which will help you locate the animals you're looking for.

Interactive zoo

There's more to the Toronto Zoo than just walking and spying on animals. At the entrance, take a few seconds to check out the day's schedule for feedings and encounters with animal keepers.

Over 70 keepers take care of the animals; many of them meet visitors daily. From them, you'll learn the animals' names, how long they've been at the zoo, what and how much they eat and any other questions the children might have.

Kesho Park is beautiful and much more interactive than the rest of the zoo. Large bay windows allow you to watch the animals through rock walls. Along the trail, kids can go right inside a large baobab tree, peek inside a termite mound, look at footprints, spy zebras and touch elephant tusks. The Park entrance is a 15-minute walk from the admission gate.

Another place where kids can stretch their muscles is the Children's Web, a playground five minutes away from the zoo entrance. That's where you can sometimes watch a free flying bird demonstration and catch a pony ride for an additional fee.

You can try a camel ride for $3. The ride schedule is between 11 am and 3 pm every day between Victoria Day and Labour Day and on weekends only during the rest of the year (weather permitting). They take place along the Camel Trail, located a 20-minute walk from the admission gate. Every day (during summer hours), try to locate the Touch Tables in the four big pavilions. They allow you to touch skulls, furs, feathers and more.

The Conservation Connection Centre (located beside the **Indomalaya** pavilion) goes one step further and offers hands-on activities: Computer Corner, Kid's Corner, Pondering Pond, Bat-Box building and a resource library.

Indoor zoo

The **Conservation Connection Centre**, along with the **Malayan Woods**, **Indomalaya**, **Africa**, **Americas** and **Australasia** pavilions, make it possible to spend most of your visit indoors. With their jungles and tropical surroundings, they offer a great outing during rainy days.

Personally, I really like these pavilions because they're enclosed spaces. Animals are within arm's reach... and so are the kids!

In the **Indomalaya** pavilion, have a close look into the amazingly intelligent eyes of the orangutan. In **Americas**, children are fascinated by the incessant moves of the lively otters. In **Australasia**, you meet eye to eye with a Tasmanian Devil.

Inside the **Africa** pavilion awaits the huge gorilla, and a chance for the kids to see what Timon the Meerkat and Rafiki the Mandrill (from the Lion King movie) look like in real life. Don't miss the intriguing (and very ugly) naked mole rats, which can be observed in their cross-sectioned maze of tunnels.

The Round the World Tour trail encompasses them all, including the outdoor polar bear pool with a wonderful underwater viewing window. Right off this trail, near the restaurant, you'll find another great attraction: the Fur Seal pool.

TIPS (fun for 2 years +)

• The **Zoomobile** (a trackless train) runs through the zoo in 45 minutes, but you may get off along the ride and hop back on later until you reach your return point. Children consider it a great attraction in itself. Beware, you can only buy **Zoomobile** tickets by the Gift Shop. I suggest you catch it in the morning before lineups form. It runs daily from Victoria Day until Canadian Thanksgiving ($3/person).
• The restaurant by the gorilla den is open all year round. Other snack bars are open during the summer throughout the site.
• The Zoo Gift Shop is huge and filled with affordable animal related items.
• Call to find out about the Nestlé Toddle for Tots in September, Halloween and Easter activities, March Break specials and Christmas Treats Walk.

NEARBY ATTRACTION
Petticoat Creek C.A. (10-min.).... p. 132

INFORMATION	**East**
Toronto Zoo • Scarborough (416) 392-5900 www.torontozoo.com	of downtown 25-min.

Schedule: Open year-round. Open from 9 am to 7:30 pm from Victoria Day to Labour Day; from 9:30 am to 4:30 pm between mid-October until mid-March; from 9 am to 6 pm the rest of the year. The last admission is one hour before closing time.

Admission: $12/adults, $9/seniors, $7/4-11 years, FREE for children 3 years and under. Parking is $5. (Prices are subject to change without notice.)

Directions: Take Hwy 401 eastbound to Scarborough, take exit 389, then go north on Meadowvale Road and follow the signs.

FORSYTHE FAMILY FARMS

Come to your senses

See the multicoloured flower baskets carpeting the market entrance and the meticulously placed products on the decorated displays. Smell the delicious warm pies and the smooth stacks of hay. Touch the apple turnovers fresh out of the oven, the goats' soft ears and the sheep's moist nostrils (in that order). Taste the golden honey, the candied apples and apple butter and hear the children laugh in the playground. You're at **Forsythe Family Farms**.

This farm-market isn't only a cornucopia of farm products; it also goes to great lengths to make us return to nature, thus captivating our five senses. Everything you could hope for in a farm can be found here, for the children's enjoyment… and for grown-ups too!

When we arrived at Forsythe Farms, we were struck by the beauty of the facilities and by the large, rustic market. The first thing my son and his friend noticed was an old tractor. Then there was the little toy house, the wooden train, the hay barn and the shed sheltering pigs, goats, hens, rabbits, turkeys and sheep, all within arm's reach.

When we visited in October, there was a maze carved into a two-acre cornfield, inside of which people were invited to get lost.

Farther along, a decorated slide and a pony-shaped swing made from a recycled tire helped to entertain the little ones while we waited for the cart ride leading to **The Enchanted Forest**.

A ten-minute cart ride brought us to the entrance of a tiny forest, where we were greeted by a funny face painted on a tree. A few wagons are put at the disposal of visitors at the edge of the forest.

Lovely paths carpeted with twigs criss-cross the woods. From time to time they reveal scenes from several popular fairy tales.

The characters made of carved and painted wood are well crafted, but their effect is rather static, except for a few which are quite lively and realistic. For little ones, the simple act of taking a stroll in the woods is impressive in itself. I suggest to those accompanying bigger kids that they ask them to identify the depicted fairy tales.

After the return cart ride, I advise you to accompany your little Sunday farmers to the straw maze that you enter through the mouth of a pumpkin. It leads to a huge mound of hay, in which I threw myself before joining a hay fight with our friends.

This activity was a great ending to our visit and allowed our children to burn off their remaining energy. Since my last visit, the owners have added a tricycle track for the kids' enjoyment.

Before you leave, consider buying one of the Farm's delicious pies. They are so good!

TIPS (fun for 2 years +)

• You can walk with a stroller to **The Enchanted Forest**.
• Call to find out about fruit picking, Halloween and Christmas activities.

INFORMATION | North

Forsythe Family Farms
· Unionville
(905) 887-1087

of Toronto
30-min.

Schedule: Open the first weekend of May until December 24, from around 9 am to 5 pm (variable hours depending on crop). The farm is open weekends only in May, daily from early June to October 31st and in December. **The Enchanted Forest** activity is open on weekend only from May until mid-November, weather permitting.
Admission: Weekend admission to the Fun area is $3/2 to 12 years and $2/adults. Weekday admission is $1/person.
Directions: 10539, Kennedy Road., Unionville. Take Hwy 404 northbound, exit Major Mackenzie eastbound, take Kennedy Rd. northbound.

NEARBY ATTRACTIONS
Toronto Zoo (15-min.).................. p. 19
Bruce's Mill C. A. (15-min.)......... p. 133

Rabbits, monkeys, bears and more at Jungle Cat World (see page 28).

PUCK'S FARM

The real thing

Only 45 minutes away from Toronto is a place where parents guide their children on a pony ride around the duck pond and robust draft horses lead passengers on a hay wagon for a tour of the hilly countryside. There, you will also find hens roaming free, cows getting milked and goats being fed.

Puck's Farm is a site where you can wander freely while giving children the opportunity to experience a real day at the farm. Hens' droppings and the multitude of flies add a touch of reality to the experience!

It was corn-picking season when we visited and ears of corn, picked by the visitors, were cooking in huge bubbling cauldrons and were to be eaten on the premises. We thought it was quite exotic to roam inside a 2-metre-high cornfield! Other pick-your-own crops such as peas, raspberries, pumpkins, wild flowers and gourds are offered at different times depending on the weather.

You will find a large barn with familiar animals. You can attend a cow milking session (a few lucky ones will even experience this hands-on!). In the outside barn, you can pet lambs, cows and goats. You can take a ride on a horse-drawn cart that takes you through a picture-perfect countryside.

The admission fee includes the many activities offered, such as a cedar bush maze, singing performances and pony rides. The pony ride delighted my young cowboy and it is unquestionably the best I've seen. Here, no sorry lads turning endlessly around a minuscule carousel. Ponies travel along a path bordering a pond.

Pink pig races are offered on weekends. Puck's Farm installed a track specifically for this attraction. At 1 pm and 3 pm on Saturdays and Sundays, visitors encourage two large hogs to run around it, and they quickly oblige.

TIPS (fun for 2 years +)

• I suggest you take along a picnic but watch out for the hens as they'll keep an eye on your food. It's part of the fun!
• You can purchase hot dogs, as well as juice and ice cream. There is also a small boutique that sells preserves and various jams.
• On rainy days, it is difficult to manoeuvre strollers on the muddy terrain. The sticky mud can suck boots in and may curb your appreciation of Puck's Farm's many activities, otherwise so enjoyable on a drier day. Better to check ground conditions the day of your visit.
• Call to find out about special events at Halloween and Easter. The Farm also offers a party package.

NEARBY ATTRACTIONS
South Simcoe Railway (15-min.) p. 66
Albion Hills C. A. (20-min.).......... p. 133

INFORMATION
North
of Toronto
45-min.

Puck's Farm
• Schomberg
(905) 939-7036
www.pucksfarm.com

Schedule: Open from Easter to Halloween on weekends and daily from July 1st, from 10 am to 4 pm.

Admission: (taxes not included) $7 per person, FREE for children under 2 years old. Gives unlimited access to all activities.

Directions: Take Hwy 400 northbound, then take exit 55 to reach Hwy 9 westbound, toward Schomberg. The farm sits 1 mile south of Hwy 9, on Concession Road 11.

BOWMANVILLE ZOO

Please feed the animals

"Not in your mouth!" For the umpteenth time, my friend catches her little one as he is about to eat an animal treat. True, the biscuits in the greasy brown paper bag do look very appetizing. Undoubtedly, the Bowmanville Zoo gives its residents the royal treatment.

Unlike the Toronto Zoo, Bowmanville's private zoo (the oldest in North America) gives visitors the opportunity to feed most of the animals, much to the delight of children. In fact, without supervision, kids would likely give their entire feed bag to the hungry and plump little goats that await them in the first compound located across the bridge.

TIPS (fun for 1 year +)

• A board at the entrance indicates the day's performances and other demonstration schedules.
• Elephant rides are offered for $4. A few mechanical rides for the very young are located near the entrance. They are included with the admission fee.
• We had a picnic under the trees, but there is an air-conditioned snack bar near the entrance, equipped with washrooms, tables and an aquarium to entertain visitors. A well-stocked boutique offers all sorts of animal-related gadgets.
• In December, the zoo presents some 30 narrated performances of the Holy Night in Bethlehem, taken from the animals perspective, featuring more than 50 animals!

I recommend a minimum of one feed bag per child (sold at the entrance for $1).

The Bowmanville Zoo also contrasts with its big brother by its smaller size (42 acres compared to 710 acres at Toronto Zoo), and a more modest sampling of animals (only 220 animals). The upswing however is the convenience of touring the zoo in a single visit and greater interaction with animals.

The broad paths that criss-cross the zoo are generally well shaded by the bordering mature trees; a real plus on hot summer days. There is a lovely country feel to the site. We began our tour with the parrots, camels, reptiles, monkeys and llamas. We then crossed a small bridge, over a river, that brought us to the elephants, lions and zebras.

Daily performances involving lions, elephants or the many other kinds of animals are presented in the indoor Animatheatre. Animal encounters also take place in and around an outdoor cage.

There are also bisons, various kinds of cervidaes, large birds with impressive calls, intriguing large rodents and roaming peacocks, geese and ducks. A separate open enclosure provides refuge to many fallow deer who rest there when not otherwise moving freely around the site.

INFORMATION	East
Bowmanville Zoo • **Bowmanville** **(905) 623-5655** www.bowmanvillezoo.com	of Toronto 45-min.

 Schedule: Open daily from 10 am, May-September and weekends only in October; closes at 6 pm. July and August; closing time varies from 4 pm to 6 pm the rest of the season.
Admission: $11.50/adults, $8.75/seniors & students,$6/2 to 12 years. (Lower rates weekdays prior to July 1st and during September and October.
Directions: 340 King St. E. (Hwy 2), Bowmanville. Hwy 401 east, exit 432 (Liberty St. northbound). Take King St. eastbound, (the zoo is located on the north side).

NEARBY ATTRACTIONS
Jungle Cat World (15-min.) ...... p. 28
Pettycoat Creek C.A. (15-min.)... p. 132

SPRINGRIDGE FARM

pies, tarts, cookies, muffins, cakes, breads, hot soups and delicious sandwiches. All of which you can eat sitting atop large barrels.

Everyday, young visitors can climb the haystack or enter the open mouth of a witch that leads to a corn maze they can explore. And they can feed the greedy sheep, goats, hens and roosters. They can play with the trucks in the large sandbox, climb up the old tractor and fly down the slide. All this for free.

Most weekends you can, for a fee, take a pony ride or a tour of the property on a tractor-drawn cart. A section of the farmland is elevated giving you a postcard perfect panoramic view.

Happy ending

Less than a 15-minute drive from other attractions in the Milton and Guelph regions (mentioned in this guide), you will find Springridge Farm on the way back to Toronto. It is ideal to loosen little legs, grab a snack and finish off your outing nicely.

Springridge's general store far exceeds what you would expect from a farm market. Inside the pleasantly decorated market you'll find a broad selection of seasonal decorative garden accessories, small toys, preserves and, best of all: excellent

TIPS (fun for 1 year +)
• Springridge closes at 5 pm. You will want to leave nearby attractions no later than 3 pm if you wish to include it in your itinerary.
• "Pick-your-own strawberries" starts mid-June, while "Pick-your-own raspberries" begins early July. During picking season, the farm opens at 8 am. You can call for a crop report.
• Every year, the farm hosts a Christmas Open House around mid-November, including gingerbread making, special entertainment and Santa Claus visit.
• Call to find out more about the farm's Birthday Party Package, Halloween and Christmas activities.

NEARBY ATTRACTIONS

INFORMATION **West** of Toronto 45-min.
Springridge Farm
• **Milton**
(905) 878-4908
www.springridgefarm.com

 Schedule: Open daily from May until Christmas, 9 am to 5 pm.
Admission: FREE (some fees may apply to activities).
 Directions: 7256 Bell School Line, Milton. Take Hwy 401, exit Guelph Line south, follow signs on Derry Rd. and Bell School Line.

JUNGLE CAT WORLD

Mommy is there!!!

"What's she doing?" a girl is cooing to a couple of tame tigers in a back cage, as her friend the keeper cleans their main cage. The big "kitties" brush their backs against the wired fence, allowing the girl to touch their beautiful fur. Then they engage in a friendly fight. Intimacy is the operative word in this privately owned zoo, which is one of a few to be accredited by the Canadian Association of Zoological Parks and Aquariums.

Visitors are welcomed to Jungle Cat World by the strident "Hello" of a real parrot. A cage, located close to the zoo entrance, generally houses the "baby" of the moment. When I visited for the first time in 1996, I was surprised to discover a German Shepherd pup and a baby lion cohabiting like the best of friends.

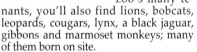

During my most recent visit, there was a young leopard gnawing a stuffed teddy. At that visit, we particularly enjoyed the otters and the small rabbit enclosure. Generally, the cages are relatively small, except those of the Siberian tigers (with its large pond) and the white wolves. However, I saw grizzly bears, wolves and tigers squabble happily. Amongst the zoo's many tenants, you'll also find lions, bobcats, leopards, cougars, lynx, a black jaguar, gibbons and marmoset monkeys; many of them born on site.

Jungle Cat World also features a small playground with free roaming deer, pigmy goats, donkeys, sheep and peacocks. There was even a goat interested in joining my kids in the turnstile! You can purchase a bag of grains ($2 a bag) to feed the animals.

TIPS (fun for 2 years +)

• Felines stay put during summer's hot days. However, count on feeding sessions every day at 1:30 pm to see them in action.
• The best way to view the marmoset monkeys is to kneel at their level while they stand on the bottom of their cage. When we visited, they stared curiously with their head bent to one side then the other, at the colourful soother in my daughter's mouth!
• Hot dogs and snacks are the only selection you'll find at the zoo snack bar. I recommend you eat at the New Dutch Oven instead. It is a family restaurant located across from the zoo.

NEARBY ATTRACTIONS

INFORMATION

Jungle Cat World
• Orono
(905) 983-5016
www.junglecatworld.com

East of Toronto 55-min.

Schedule: Open year-round, 7 days a week 10 am to 5 pm.

Admission: $9.50/adults, $7/seniors and students, $4.25/2-13 years, FREE for children 2 years and under.
Directions: 3667 Consession 6, Orono. Take Hwy 401 to Hwy 35/115 (exit 436), 11 km north to Taunton Road.

KORTRIGHT WATERFOWL PARK

Quacky corner

At the Kortright Waterfowl Park, in Guelph, the flock of birds walking towards us believes my son is Dr. Doolittle... Kids understand they hold power in their hands while they give out golden grains. If we manage to restrain their first impulse (giving out all the food at once), we'll easily spend an hour observing the feathered population's frolicking.

At the end of the winding boardwalk, a path leads to the park's entrance: a door cut into a high, wire mesh fence. We're here to observe all classes of web-footed birds that we already hear quacking from afar.

Following the concert, we head for the meeting point of all free-roaming species: the big pond. Some birds were adopted by the Centre and had feathers removed to prevent them from flying away. Other wild birds came here on their own free will. Rare specimens stay confined in pens.

Like any other Torontonians, we were a bit blasé as we watched the flock of Canada geese greeting us. However, we found their friends, the large black swans, quite ravishing. When stretched out, the tallest one's big muscular neck was the same height as my five-year old son. I was quite impressed!

Each species gives out a very different call: from the trumpet blaring out a wild jazz tune to the small toy horn. When they all compete to attract our attention, the result is a joyous cacophony.

Beaks come in all styles: green, pink, red or black, long, short or curled up. Feet, song and sizes are as varied. I had no idea that there were so many types of ducks and geese. Kortright houses over 90 different species; though not all are on display to visitors.

"Cow! Cow!" cried out my little one (she uses the word "cow" to point out any four-footed, large animal). Then, we caught a glimpse of a deer family hiding in the undergrowth. We spot them in different locations, always alerted by my quick-eyed daughter. We also saw a pudgy groundhog and rabbits.

TIPS (fun for 1 year +)
• At the entrance, bags of corn (the only food allowed) are sold. I recommend that you buy at least one per child. It's great to watch the birds scheme while they approach us or protect their territory. Certain ones are shy; others have eaten out of my young ornithologist's hand.
• In late spring (usually by mid-May) we can admire cygnets, goslings and ducklings! Call the park to find out when they're out.

NEARBY ATTRACTIONS

INFORMATION	West
Kortright Waterfowl Park **· Guelph** **(519) 824-6729**	**of Toronto** **60-min.**

 Schedule: Weekends and Holidays, from March 1st until October 31st, from 10 am to 5 pm.
Admission: $2.50/adults, $2/seniors and students, $1/4 to 14 years, FREE for children under 4.
Directions: 305 Niska Road, Guelph. Take Hwy 401, exit toward Hwy 6 North. Continue on 6 North, turn left (westbound) on Kortright Street. Niska Street is on the right.

AFRICAN LION SAFARI

Close encounters of the animal kind

Go figure why children are so attracted to animals! They're happy visiting a traditional zoo, but become literally ecstatic when encountering the fantastic opportunities offered by African Lion Safari. The park is huge and offers the unique opportunity to drive through the animals' living quarters, with your car windows as the only screen between your children and the animals.

African Lion Safari houses over 1000 exotic animals and birds of 132 species. When we rode through the seven large game reserves we first encountered big birds such as emus. We then watched sleeping lions that didn't lift an eyebrow; the tigers were just as lethargic. The whole scenery lacked action... then a crowd of baboons started to jump on our car!

If you're able to live with the idea of a monkey's "little present" decorating the hood of your car, I strongly recommend using your own vehicle instead of the zoo's bus. Children become delirious with joy with baboons perched on the windshield. Having tried both, I see many disadvantages to the bus option.

TIPS (fun for 2 years +)
• Don't forget the bathing suits!
• The park's restaurant and gift shop are well stocked and affordable.
• There's a campground beside the park. Its customers benefit from a discount on the park admission fee.

First, you don't control the amount of time spent watching each animal (the Safari Tour Bus ride takes approximately 1 hr 15-min.; in your own vehicle, it lasts as long as you please).

Second, the bus offers little grip for the monkeys, while cars make comfortable perches.

You'll meet among others: a few tall giraffes (rather impressive from up close), some albino rhinoceros, zebras and antelopes. Then, you can witness the elephant's bath, watch shows by parakeets and birds of prey and see other trained animal performances. You can cross the pond on board the small boat named **African Queen**, ride the small train and pet the animals at the **Pets Corner**.

In the summer, children will enjoy playing in the water games at the **Misumu Bay Wet Play & Jungle Playground**, located close to the restaurant's terrace.

(Photo: African Lion Safari)

INFORMATION
African Lion Safari
• **Cambridge**
1 (800) 461-9453
www.lionsafari.com

West of Toronto 75-min.

Schedule: Open daily end of April to Canadian Thanksgiving from 10 am to 5:30 pm during the summer; closes at 4 pm during spring and fall. The game reserves open at 10 am. The grounds remain open 90-min after the ticket booth and game reserves are closed. Times for the various shows differ on weekdays and weekends.

Admission: (taxes not included) $18.95/13-64 years, $15.95/seniors, $13.95/3-12 years, FREE for children 2 years and under. Tour bus costs approx. $5 extra per person.

Directions: Hwy 401 West, past Milton, take exit 299 (Hwy 6) southbound for 14 km and turn right on Safari Road.

NEARBY ATTRACTIONS

THE BIG APPLE

Have a bite!

While I'm busy taking a picture of my children having fun at the Big Apple playground, I feel something applying gentle pressure on my feet. Looking down, I discover a cute bunny chewing calmly on my straw handbag!

The Big Apple, located on the south side of Highway 401, is worth the stop when driving in the corridor between Montreal and Toronto.

The apple dessert counter inside the major building will make your mouth water: cookies, muffins, tarts, dumplings, buns… Large windows allow visitors to look inside the kitchen, where the bakers are in action all dressed in white. The outdoor playground is fun and the bunny rabbits are adorable. If you look closely, you can see more than twenty of them roaming freely on the site.

The Big Apple, well, is big! It stands more than 10 metres high and you can climb to the top from inside, while viewing a few apple-theme displays.

Children want to reach the tiny balcony located at the top of the Apple. The scenery offers nothing outstanding, but you can see far away.

For $2, you may rent clubs in the gift shop to play miniature golf at the foot of the Apple.

Small dens are inhabited by deer, sheep, llamas and pigs. They can be fed with grains from vending machines. Behind them, you will find a few small trails by a pond; enough to stretch small legs before continuing your journey.

TIPS (fun for 2 years +)

• You can have a meal in the huge fast-food restaurant but the tasty apple desserts and snacks are the main reason to stop at the Big Apple.
• Think of bringing baby carrots so children can enjoy offering a real treat to the rabbits.
• The big gift shop is filled with Canadian souvenirs and trinkets.

INFORMATION	East
The Big Apple • Colborne (905) 355-2574 www.biggestapple.com	of Toronto 90-min.

Schedule: Open year-round from 7:30 am to 7 pm (closes at 9 pm from April 1 to October 31)
Admission: FREE
Directions: Big Apple Drive, Colborne. Take Hwy 401, exit 497 southbound, then Big Apple Drive.

BUTTERFLY CONSERVATORY

Butterfly-friendly attraction

My little naturalist miraculously stops moving for a minute, hoping that one of the two thousand butterflies in the greenhouse will mistake him for a flower and land on him. A woman, looking through her camera, waits for the perfect moment to snap a picture, unaware that a wonderful specimen is resting on her head. I take my time to capture (on film) a superb green and black butterfly standing 10 centimetres away from me.

The visit begins with the viewing of a short film. It is followed by a leisurely walk around the greenhouse for as long as we want. The conservatory layout includes trees, bushes and flower clumps, as well as a small waterfall. The hot and humid air contributes to the overall exotic feel of the place.

The beautiful winged insects are quite tame. In truth, they were born in this environment and have grown accustomed to the crowds that regularly and respectfully, visit the hothouse.

We are told that nearly fifty butterfly species live freely at the Niagara Butterfly Conservatory. I couldn't tell most of them apart, yet I saw at close range all sorts of exotic kinds including blue, black, red, yellow and orange ones. Here and there, fruit plates are left for the hungry butterflies so that we may admire them while they eat. We can also observe their cocoons in each phase of development, suspended from the shelving of a large window with openings. A few iguanas share the space!

Don't miss the interactive learning stations in the entrance hall. There, children will try to connect wings to the appropriate caterpillar, look through glasses that recreate butterflies'eyesight and observe specimens through a microscope. You can end your outing with a visit to adjacent outdoor gardens (the Niagara Parks Butterfly Conservatory sits at the centre of a botanical garden), have a bite at the local snack bar or browse in the large gift shop.

TIPS (fun for 4 years +)
• Purchase your tickets as soon as you arrive as only then will the time of your visit be assigned (often one hour later). Timed ticket reservation can be made in advance by phone.
• Washrooms at the conservatory are less busy than those at the snack bar.
• Niagara Parks Greenhouse, upstream from the Falls, boasts exotic free flying birds, waterfalls and pools (FREE admission).

NEARBY ATTRACTIONS
Marineland (20-min.).................. p. 33
Niagara Falls (10-min.).............. p. 104

INFORMATION
Niagara Parks Butterfly Conservatory
• **Niagara Falls**
1-877-642-7275 or (905) 371-0254
www.niagaraparks.com

Niagara Region 90-min.

 Schedule: Open year-round daily from 9 am to 9 pm during the summer. Variable closing hours the rest of the year. (Last admission one hour prior to closing time.)

Admission: $8/adults, $4/ 6 to 12 years, FREE for 5 years and under.

Directions: Take Q.E.W. toward Niagara Falls; exit at Hwy 420. Continue 6km on the Niagara Parkway northbound.

MARINELAND

Not just another fish story...

As soon as kids try to feed one of the hundreds of deer Marineland is swarming with, they're swept away amidst a sea of white spots with dozens of wet noses and velvety antlers tickling their faces.

When you think of Marineland, the first thought that comes to mind is the sight of killer whales splashing the crowd. Yet this attraction offers plenty of other activities too, making for a great outing with children: a huge fish-feeding pond, a bear pit, a deer park, rides, a roller coaster and of course, the new pool allowing a closer view of the killer whales.

Get an early start

In July and August, the site opens at 9 am (10 am for the rest of the season). If you can, try to get there no later than 10 am to avoid unpleasant lineups, especially if you want to try the rides.

As soon as you arrive, head for the theatre where the next performance will be held. Schedules for the shows are posted at the site's entrance. It's better to get there 15 minutes before performances begin.

Killer whale and sea lion shows are presented in the **King Waldorf Theatre**, left of the entrance. The **Aquarium Theatre** is located on the right side of the entrance. It features a show starring sea lions and a dolphin (Yep! It seems Marineland is now down to only one dolphin!).

While waiting for the killer whale act to begin, I asked myself how I would succeed in keeping my young thrill-seeker in his place. To my great relief, a clown started a series of excellent antics,

at the expense of several members of the audience, to help us pass the time while waiting. The animal show itself lasted approximately half an hour.

Inside their glass basin, the killer whales are gigantic. The first sight I had of them left me standing open-mouthed. It is incredible to watch these impressive forces of nature perform their number in unison. However, the best way to watch these mastodons is to go to **Friendship Cove**, Marineland's new basin, with fabulous underwater viewing windows. For above water viewing, it's also surrounded by walkways. You might even get a chance to touch the whales. **Friendship Cove** is located a 15-minute walk away from the admission gate.

After doing the rounds of all the other activities on site, we wanted to end our day by watching the dolphin show. Unfortunately, the theatre was full. If this happens to you, don't despair! You can still see the dolphin perform thanks to the wide underwater viewing windows located in the basement of the theatre. Freshwater aquariums are also located at this level.

Watching from the underwater viewing windows, you can appreciate the dolphin's power and precision as it dives over and over again, brushing against the bottom without hitting it after having completely propelled itself out of the water.

cepted the hand-off before I could make it and my young zoologist disappeared among the animals. It's best to take children 4 years and under in your arms before the invasion begins.

When heading towards these attractions, you'll pass by the **Kiddie Rides** area. It includes a small roller coaster, especially designed for the younger crowd, that we really enjoyed. There's a Viking boat carousel for the whole family, a Ferris wheel and the Space Avenger.

Beyond **Friendship Cove**, you can find more elaborate rides: the Sky Hawk (for children over 32" accompanied by an

One, two, three, GO!

There are three points of interest not to be missed at Marineland: the fish pond, the bear pit and the deer park. For the best effect, visit them in that order. A detailed map is given to visitors at the entrance.

At each of these areas, it's possible to buy food ($1.25/cup) and feed the animals. Children love these interactive activities.

The fish are enormous. From the bridge, you can see them well and you can even touch them if you stand on the small wharf! Inside the pit, there are several bears. They greedily swallow the miniature marshmallows that people throw into their mouths.

You'll be surprised by the number of deer greeting you at the deer park entrance, but most of the 500 animals are at the back, close to the stand where deer food is for sale.

When the deer see someone getting close to that stand, they spread the word to others and they all press against the surprised buyer. I was never able to transfer grains to my son's hand so he could feed the deer himself. They inter-

adult), the Wave Swinger, the Hurricane Cove (both for 42"+) and the Flying Dragon (46"+).

Close to the bear pit, you can get a good shake at the Magic ride (46"+). The huge Dragon Mountain roller coaster (48"+) is located a bit farther, close to the Red Deer, Elk-Wapiti and Bison pens.

Access to all rides is included in the admission fee.

TIPS (fun for 3 years +)

• Before you arrive, be aware that Marineland's parking lot is set up lengthwise. If you're parked at one of its extremities, you'll have to walk more than five minutes before reaching the park entrance. Furthermore, Marineland is vast. You'll require a stroller for young children. Dolphin-shaped strollers can be rented on site for $6 a day.

• There's barely any shade on the Marineland site. Don't forget water bottles, hats and sunscreen!

• When we arrived, the theatre where the killer whale show was held seemed full. We walked along the amphitheatre's edge and reached a ramp that lead to the top of the auditorium and we found a place in one of the last rows (where we had a good view of the show).

• By the way, if you sit in the first ten rows, bring a change of clothes and hide your camera!

• If the waiting line seems long, I advise you to avoid the Space Avenger in the **Kiddie Rides** section. This ride's boarding procedure is longer than for other activities and the ride is quite short. This can be extremely frustrating after a 20-minute wait.

• Don't do what my friend and I tried: to prop our children's caps up on their heads in order to make them reach the required height for a certain ride! The employee took a good 30 seconds to measure them carefully, then refused them access without batting an eye. You should have seen the two contrite mothers, tearing their sobbing little ones away from the ride they had anticipated for 15 minutes... It was a pathetic sight!

• For lunch, expect to pay about $7 for a hamburger with fries at the Marineland cafeteria. You'll find large indoor and outdoor areas with tables, perfect for pic-

nics. Not far from the eating area, a playground gives little ones a chance to digest their meals.

• The gift shop is huge and filled with small souvenirs. And by the entrance, there's a noisy (but air-conditioned) video arcade, with games galore.

INFORMATION	Niagara
Marineland • **Niagara Falls** **(905) 356-9565** **www.marinelandcanada.com**	**Region** **90-min.**

Schedule: The park opens from May until mid-October. Amusement rides operate from Victoria Day weekend until Thanksgiving weekend. From May to mid-May and beginning September to mid-October, open from 10 am to 4 pm, from Mid-May to end of June, open until 5 pm, July and August, open from 9 am to 6 pm. All park activities remain in operation until dusk, after the admission gate closes.

Admission: (taxes not included) From the end of June until beginning of September:$27.95/10-59 years, $24.50/5 to 9 years and seniors, FREE for children 4 years and under. Admission fee costs $4 less at beginning and end of the season and approx. $12 less in the first and last weeks when amusement rides are closed.

Directions: 7657 Portage Road, Niagara Falls.Take Q.E.W. in the direction of Niagara Falls, then follow signs.

❤ Ontario Renaissance Festival

With over fifty actors at a time on the site, there is bound to be action. They interact with you while continuing to play their part as they stroll around the village. Add to this shows, theatre plays, musicians, games, human chess match and knight challenges.

(see page 44)

FESTIVALS & EVENTS

HARBOURFRONT CENTRE

First, there is the Harbourfront Centre for adults, with its ambitious programs including dance, music and theatre festivals, conferences and visual arts exhibits. At all times you can view at no cost an eclectic selection of art works at the **York Quay Gallery** and along the main building's corridors. The **Power Plant** is wholly dedicated to exhibits of modern art entered with admission fee.

For the more inquisitive mind, the **Craft Studio** allows visitors to watch artists in action as they are crafting glass, metal, ceramics or textiles. Children are generally impressed by the glassblower's prowess with the large red ball coming out of the oven's belly, and its patient transformation into a shapely vase with handles.

Then, there is the Harbourfront Centre for children, which prides itself on helping children become familiar to the world of culture and the arts. They offer throughout the year: Cushion Concerts, Children International Milk Festival, Toronto Festival of Storytelling, March Break and Summer Camps, Canadian Thanksgiving festival, New Year's Eve celebration and a host of cultural fairs.

A family affair

Harbourfront Centre sits on the edge of the water. Its waterfront terrace with panoramic view of Lake Ontario on one side and CN Tower on the other, the long promenade along the piers with its many choices of harbour cruises, and most of all, the over 4000 large and small events taking place year-round, explain the site's huge popularity. In a word, it is one of the most gorgeous spots in Toronto.

Canada Day is reason enough for special activities during a 3-day party.

During the summer weekends, visitors will sample different cultures when looking at the crafts at the **International Marketplace** and tasting the World cuisine at the **World Cafe** near the Harbourfront Centre Concert Stage.

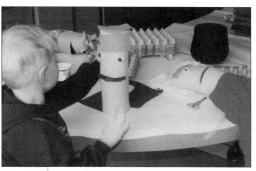

HarbourKids Creative Workshops

After an hour and a half of intensive work, we brought home numerous masterpieces. They bore witness to my little artist's patience and to the originality of the craft ideas. These activities are offered on Sundays and holidays by **HarbourKids Creative Workshops**.

No need to pre-register for these workshops; simply show up. The young artists touch everything, supervision is as hands-off as possible and you'll see lovely creations emerge from their little hands.

On the day of our visit, the kids made and decorated a cardbox hat with a large rim, some funny masks in the shape of flowers, stars and birds and for the more ambitious, two impressive puppets made

from foam, recycled wires and clothing. Every week, a new and inspiring program is offered. The most original crafts I noticed were: "piggy checkers" game, pet collars, moose-call makers, rain sticks, snow globes, tissue paper "stained glass" and jester hats and shoes.

As much as possible, proposed crafts coincide with special events happening at Harbourfront Centre.

The very young will always find a little something to do in the many activities offered. However, it is around age 3, with adult assistance, that they will be better able to complete a project. The program always includes a more elaborate activity for older children.

TIPS (fun for 3 years +)

• When the canoes and kayaks of the **Harbourfront Canoe School** are not used for the summer classes, it is possible to rent them to paddle on the 18-inch deep pond, at the cost of $5 for 30 minutes. Kids love to row as close as possible to the fountain!

• The **Lakeside EATS** terrace is heaven during the warmer days. The restaurant's menu at the counter is tasty and affordable.

• A cute fenced playground is located by the water.

• **Queen's Quay Terminal** just east of Harbourfront Centre is a small and beautiful shopping centre worth a visit. It includes various specialty stores: dolls, musical boxes, kites, toys, candy and more, along with a food court on the second floor.

INFORMATION	Downtown
Harbourfront Centre	Toronto
(416) 973-3000	5-min.
www. harbourfront.on.ca	

 Schedule: Open year-round; variable opening and closing hours depending on the events.

 HarbourKids Creative Workshops are offered year-round (except in January) every Sunday and Holiday day and most Saturdays, from noon to 5 pm.

Admission: FREE ground admission, $2/person to participate in the HarbourKids workshops.

Directions: 235 Queen's Quay West (west of York Street), Toronto.

CARAVAN

Around the world in 9 days

Visiting any of Caravan's pavilions makes anyone a tourist in Toronto. You get to taste food you can't name and buy the crafts you would buy, were you to visit the countries represented here. You also mingle with Toronto's cultural communities, each very well represented among the audience in the pavilion that showcases their heritage.

The Toronto International Festival Caravan (simply known as Caravan) has been a Toronto tradition for over 30 years. During Caravan, each pavilion (over 30 of them) marks the event by selling special foods. Some we recognize and others, we don't: Rasanali (boiled cheese soaked in sugar syrup with rosewater), melomakarono (dough fingers flavoured with orange juice), tulumbi (decadent batter in honey sauce), pavlova (meringue and kiwi cake). So many exotic desserts to discover!

Caravan is best for children with

strong feelings for dance and music since these are the main attractions offered in all the pavilions. Some performers are as young as two and quite cute to watch. Others are seasoned professionals who will delight you with exotic dances involving Ukranian's red boots, Polynesian's grass skirts, Filipino bamboo Tinikling, flamenco's castanets and belly-dancing's bells.

Young travellers at heart, with a taste for geography, will appreciate the passport to be stamped.

More activities are on the program in the different pavilions. During my visit, children particularly enjoyed the Ukranian pavilion Odessa, where they could learn to paint their own egg using wax in the old-fashioned way. Everybody loved to join in the circle of dance at the Native pavilion! I thought the sari demonstration at the New Delhi pavilion was fascinating.

Pavilions vary from one year to the next but the festive spirit remains with over 200 shows in nine days.

TIPS (fun for 5 years +)
• The Guide to Caravan is available in advance (call the office) or during the festival at all pavilions. It lists showtimes and provides maps and TTC (public transportation) information. This is all you'll need to build your own itinerary.
• Certain pavilions are located within walking distance from each other and this allows you to plan a small itinerary. You should bring a stroller to wander around with young children.
• You can get a Caravan passport at the CN Tower. It includes maps and addresses to all of the pavilions.

INFORMATION Toronto International Festival Caravan (416) 977-0466	Toronto various locations
 	Schedule: Runs for 9 days. In 2000, from June 23 to July 1. Open from 6 pm to 11 pm on week days and from 3 pm to 11 pm on Saturdays and Sundays (late night parties at selected pavilions).

Admission: Passport gives unlimited access to all the pavilions. Cost is $20/person. 1-day passport is $10/person. FREE for children 12 years and under.
Directions: The pavilions are located all over Toronto.

TORONTO STREET FESTIVAL

Street smart!

During the Toronto Street Festival, Yonge Street transforms itself. A short section of Canada's longest street becomes traffic free and takes on the appearance of a fun fair amid trapeze artists balancing against the backdrop of skyscrapers or a large inflated dragon engulfing happy children, and people gathering around one of the many outdoor performances. The street becomes an extravagant display of colour and excitement.

When we were there, children were enjoying improvised sandboxes sitting next to a large sandcastle under construction. Nearby, professional divers were jumping off high diving boards into a small pool. At one intersection, passengers bounced on board a large inflated replica of the Titanic. At another, children bounced off sets of inflated structures.

Down the road, visitors embarked for a ride inside the elevated cabin of an Ontario Hydro truck's hydraulic arm, while others enjoyed making crafts in one of the many tents along the street.

Further down, a good selection of paying rides attracted visitors, as well as performances by acrobats and trained dogs participating in an obstacle race.

Add street performers and an impressive flow of visitors to the mix and you get a good idea of this fun-packed, high-density event. While activities change from year to year, the same spirit remains.

TIPS (fun for 3 years +)

• You would need more than one hour to walk the section of Yonge Street where activities take place. A convenient alternative is to purchase a day pass from the TTC (Toronto Transit Commission), as it gives you unlimited entry to all subway stations including those along Yonge Street.
• When we visited, most activities were free except the midway rides, for which we purchased individual tickets. Expect long line-ups for free activities.
• You will find a list of activities on-site for the two day festival.

NEARBY ATTRACTION
Mt. Pleasant Cemetery (10-min.)... p. 92

INFORMATION	**Toronto**
Toronto Street Festival	various
(416) 395-7350	locations
www.city.toronto.on.ca	

 Schedule: In 2000, the Festival is held July 7, 8 pm to 11 pm, July 8, 10 am to 11 pm, July 9, 10 am to 7 pm.

 Admission: FREE (extra charge for Midway rides).

Directions: On Yonge Street, at the intersection of King Street, Bloor Street, St. Clair Avenue, Eglinton Avenue and Lawrence Avenue (all serviced by a subway station).

SQUARE IN MOTION

Hanging around the Square

On a summer Tuesday, parents on vacation might want to pay a visit to the Kids Tuesday free concerts for children offered at Nathan Phillips Square. They come complete with arts and crafts workshops, activities and giveaways.

When we were there, a Caribbean-spirited band had transformed the square into a small "Caribana" for children. Preschoolers from daycare centres were spontaneously swinging to the music. Bigger kids were forming dance chains that criss-crossed the square and people were testing their limbo skills at the foot of the futuristic City Hall building.

Lineups were a bit long but we could decorate masks. We got hats made out of balloons and face paint to match.

My friend's outgoing daughter even ended up on stage with some other lucky kids invited to play percussion with the band. It was a perfect little outing.

Activities vary from one week to the next but you can always count on a hands-on craft and interactive show.

TIPS (fun for 3 years +)

• Nathan Phillips Square is a 5-min. walk away from the **Eaton Centre**, with its 3-storey high fountain, glass door elevators, ice cream stands and over 200 shops.
• Inside **City Hall**, you will find an intriguing model of downtown Toronto on which kids will recognize the CN Tower... and City Hall.

NEARBY ATTRACTIONS

INFORMATION Square in Motion (416) 395-7350 www.city.toronto.on.ca	Downtown Toronto 15-min.

 Schedule: In 2000, Kids Tuesday begins July 18 and ends August 8, from 11 am to 1 pm.
 Admission: FREE
Directions: Nathan Phillips
 Square, Toronto (on Queen Street West, at the corner of Bay Street).

CANADIAN NATIONAL EXHIBITION

Midway stop

With the large rides located close to the Princes' Gate, and the younger children's section, the Kids' Midway, located on the site's opposite side by Dufferin Gates, CNE is indeed a children's paradise!

To this, add special exhibitions that are bound to interest children. Year 2000 features a Cat Show, Super Dogs performances, a **Sportzone** filled with interactive extreme sports to try and a Canada 2000 pavilion to celebrate the new millenium.

When we visited, there was a great variety of rides at the **Kids' Midway**: a merry-go-round, a Ferris wheel, a small and medium-sized rollercoaster, the bumble bee, flying helicopter and planes, jeep and construction trucks that went round and round, tossing submarines, shaking strawberries, and more. Most of these rides have a maximum height requirement of 42 inches.

In this area, there are also games of dexterity for an additional cost, where children are guaranteed a prize; frankly, that's all they ask for. The **Midway** closer to the Princes' Gate is a busy place for bigger kids, with minimum height requirements of 42 to 48 inches.

Activities at **Kids' World**, located west of **Kids' Midway**, are of another kind, but equally entertaining. Amongst them, the booth from Science North (which returns yearly), is packed with widgets to touch and experiments to observe. It has a music room, equipped with the latest percussion and recording technology.

The Craft Studio attracts fervent crafters with its well-stocked locale, while the Junk Joint is the place where you can create original objects made from recycled material.

TIPS (fun for 3 years +)
• It will cost you approximately $17 to park your car on the CNE site; try neighbourhood parking on Fleet Street, east of Strachan Avenue.
• Express shuttles transport you free of charge across the site. Take advantage of this service as it easily takes 20 minutes to walk across the site.
• The **Kids' World** area is interesting for children 12 years and under. The **Kids' Midway** might not offer enough thrills for children over 8 years old. They will prefer the big **Midway**.

NEARBY ATTRACTIONS
Ontario Place (5-min.)................ p. 10
Historic Fort York (5-min.).......... p. 110

INFORMATION	Downtown
CNE	Toronto
(416) 263-3800	**15-min.**
www.theex.com	

Schedule: Open the last two weeks prior to Labour Day from 10 am to 10 pm, ends at Labour Day. The big **Midway** closes at midnight. The **Kids' World** activities close at 8 pm but kiddies rides remain open as long as there are customers.

Admission: Ground admission is $8/adults, $5/seniors and children under 6 years old, FREE for babies in arm. Midway Pass is $20/person (excluding cost of admission). It includes unlimited access to all the rides. Individual ride coupons are sold.

Directions: Exhibition Place, by the Lake Shore Boulevard West. Princes' Gate entrance on Strachan Avenue; Dufferin Gates on Dufferin Avenue.

ONTARIO RENAISSANCE FESTIVAL

Playing in the royal court...yard

Upon eyeing the size of our watermelon, the village apothecary exclaims (in renaissance English): "It's certainly not produced locally". He collects the seeds from the piece we had offered to him, anticipating their medicinal properties. A damsel, all trussed up in her bodice, interrupts our picnic claiming to have stolen the ring of King Henry VIII's new wife Queen Anne, while they were shaking hands. Before fleeing, she begs us not to breathe a word about this to anyone. Indeed, there's a lot of action at the Renaissance Festival.

In 1999, it was all about Henry VIII. In 2000, the action is built around Elizabeth I. In all, there are about fifty actors at a time on the Festival site, very well costumed and scattered in small groups throughout the village.

In old English, they shout out false confidences intended for everyone's ears. If you smile at them, they interact with you, but continue to play their part.

There's an arena of course, to go along with the spirit. Here they hold authentic jousting matches where knights, in full armour, fight one another with spears. They also hold birds-of-prey demonstrations. During our visit, public entertainers gave Molière and Shakespeare performances for the whole family. Of course, period music was much in evidence, with minstrels wandering throughout the village.

Half of the village huddles up against the edge of a shaded forest. This gives us the impression we are close to the Nottingham Forest. In these woods, a few activities included with the entrance fee can be found: an animal pen (where we petted a baby goat!), pony ride, and juggling lessons.

In the same area, some 50 artisans present their merchandise: glass blowers, blacksmith, sculptors and more. Some crafts are really eye-catching: beaded crowns made of flowers and long ribbons, butterfly wings or wooden armour to dress up as a fairy or a knight.

For a few dollars more, several other activities are offered: archery, ax and spear throw, rope ladder climbing, arm makeup and wax hand-castings. The maze isn't very interesting, but the wooden horses are a must; children four years and older will really enjoy this. They'll charge on coloured horses, spear in hand, aiming at a small ring.

The Human Chess match was by far our family's favourite activity! The "pieces" had previously been recruited from amongst the audience. The people chosen stood on a giant chessboard. Their moves were dependent on the outcome of several fights between actors, each one funnier than the last and guided by a narrator amidst general chaos.

By taking advantage of many shows, we definitely got our money's worth!

Some families, already familiar with the ways of the Festival, dress up for the occasion. We saw little knights and princesses strolling behind mothers clad in long skirts... and dads who didn't dare to be crazy and dress up!

TIPS (fun for 4 years +)

• At the entrance, a plan of the site is given out; it contains a detailed schedule of all the shows.
• Those interested in jousting should arrive at least 15 minutes before the show to have a seat in the stand, unfortunately placed right in the sun.
• Hats are a must, since more than half the site is right in the sun.
• If you don't want to spend more than the admission fee, take a deep breath and be on the defensive when you and the kids pass in front of the shops selling Renaissance articles: shields, wooden swords, flower crowns... they're all so tempting!
• Giant smoked turkey legs which taste like ham or chicken sandwiches won't necessarily appeal to young palates. When we visited, the rest of the menu offered little variety. I therefore recommend that you bring a boxed lunch.

NEARBY ATTRACTIONS

Rattray Marsh C. A. (15-min.)..... p. 98
Kelso C. A. (15-min.)................... p. 133

INFORMATION
Ontario Renaissance Festival
• Milton
1-800-734-3779
www.rennfest.com

West of Toronto 45-min.

Schedule: Weekends only starting the last weekend of July until the second weekend of September, from 10:30 am to 7 pm.
Admission: $16.95/adults, $15.50/seniors, $8/7 to 15 years, FREE for children 6 years and under.
Directions: East of Trafalgar Road, on Height Line, Milton. From Hwy 401, take exit 328, head south for 2 km, turn left on Derry Rd, continue for 1 km, then turn right on Height Line. (Alternate way: take exit 118 from the Q.E.W., head north for 11.3 km, turn right on Britannia for 1 km, then turn left on Height Line.)

❤ Cullen Gardens & Miniature Village

The village of approximately one hundred miniature buildings includes a main road, a residential area, a few estates, a large resort, secondary residences, a campground, trains, yachts, a ferry, a church and a fire station; all populated with created-to-scale citizens. Then, there is the fabulous garden, the great playground, the wading pool, the suspension bridge...

(see page 54)

INTRIGUING
BUILDINGS

CN TOWER

Up! Up! And away!

Then comes the famous ride up the elevator: it's a one-minute climb on a fair day, but it can take up to four minutes in high wind. Don't hesitate to let your children go close to the glass door. The view will leave them with an unforgettable memory.

Broaden their horizons

With kids, you have to think big and tall... as tall as the CN Tower! It's great to see them looking up over and over again, attempting to make out the top of the 550-metre high tower! It's well worth stopping at the base, just to see the great view from down there.

Arriving from Front Street, we walk over several railroad tracks via a sheltered corridor. This location is an excellent vantage point to see the sculptures of giant characters in their **Sky Dome** balconies.

Inside, before getting to the elevators, we walk across a spacious mezzanine housing fancy interactive displays, but don't think that they only contain serious information.

Have the kids take a look at the **CN Tower in Tour** display on the touch screens. They'll love to place the tower, feet in the water, beside the Rio de Janeiro Bay or better still, on the slopes of the Himalayas. They should also explore the Hop, Skip & Jump file. They'll see eccentric athletes in action: one that climbed up the Tower's 1760 steps with a pogo-stick, another one who climbed its walls without a net and those who threw themselves from the top of the Tower hang-gliding or bungee jumping!

Closer to the elevators, visual simulators located on three screens give us the impression of flying with a hang-glider, of jumping with a bungee cord or walking on a high wire.

The elevator leads to the interior observation deck, 346 m (1136 feet) from ground level, from where we can admire Lake Ontario and the four corners of the city.

Children are allowed inside the **Horizons** bar located at this level. There are not many affordable and interesting choices for kids on the menu. However, the last time I visited the Tower, we stopped to have two cafés au lait and two apple juices. The $10 we paid for these drinks seemed like an excellent investment, considering the fun we had admiring Lilliputian cars circulating on miniature highways and trying to identify Toronto's well-known buildings.

The view impressed the kids nearly as much as the tiny CN Tower-shaped sticks decorating their juice!

One floor down is the fascinating glass floor surrounded by a beautiful mural depicting a construction site in the sky.

Until the age of five, my little tightrope artist didn't show any fear while walking on the transparent floor. Now that he's getting close to six years old, he has joined the rank of grown-ups that tend to cautiously remain on the edge of the glass squares.

To all those who, like him, ask themselves how such a surface can support visitors, the designers answer that this glass floor can hold the weight of 14 large hippos! At this level, you can also access the exterior observation deck, to better feed your vertigo. We didn't feel the need to pay extra and go up to the Sky Pod. What difference can 100 metres more make?

Everybody down

To complete the outing, other activities are offered at the base of the Tower. There's an Imax movie at the Maple Leaf theatre. Other films are presented in a mini-theatre equipped with seats that move to the rhythm of the movie projected on screen. Young children will enjoy

it, but regular visitors to this type of attraction will be disappointed.

On the other hand, the arcade is pretty with its river painted on the ground and its pillars adorned with dinosaurs. Very few games are suitable for smaller children, but my little one had a great time driving the motorcycles. And he and I teamed up, frantically rowing on a rubber dinghy, while attempting to avoid dangerous situations. I sweated up a storm and we laughed the whole time.

TIPS (fun for 5 years +)
• Avoid very windy days, when access to the outside observation deck and to the Sky Pod is forbidden. Also avoid foggy days, otherwise you'll be paying a lot just to have your head in the clouds...
• For a better viewpoint of the Tower in all its loftiness, stand on the outside terrace located between the Tower and the Sky Dome.

NEARBY ATTRACTIONS

INFORMATION	Downtown

INFORMATION Downtown
CN Tower Toronto
(416) 868-6937
www.cntower.ca

Schedule: Open daily year-round: 8 am to 11 pm from April to October, shorter hours during the rest of the year.
Admission: (taxes not included) $15.99/adults, $13.99/seniors, $10.99/4-12 years, FREE for children 3 years and under. (Simulator, cinema, visit to Sky Pod and Arcade tokens are extra.)
Directions: 301 Front St. W. (corner of John St.).

MARCHÉ MÖVENPICK

Market analysis

My family and I really enjoy going out to eat, for the change of scenery and crowd immersion it provides (two reasons that suit my little explorer just fine). And there's the sheer pleasure of having someone else cook for us ("Is there another way to get what you want?" my little guy asks slightly puzzled). The uniqueness of this concept and an ideal location have made Mövenpick Market our preferred choice for a family brunch.

There are no endless waits on your chair here. Simply pick a table and venture out into the profusion of chef-manned stations, where your order will be prepared in front of you. The overall setting is bliss for the senses with its lavish displays of cooking ingredients and tempting presentations.

The sizzling sound of cooking omelettes and roasting potatoes; the freshly baked smell of danishes, small breads and warm crêpes, married to the full-bodied aroma of freshly brewed coffee that teases your nostrils; the sweet bouquet of apples mixed with the tempting smells of crisp vegetables blending with delectable sauces in a skillet; all combine in a invitingly appetizing experience. Hard to imagine a child ever getting bored in such a place!

The Market is located in the heart of **BCE Place**. The large hall (which connects Yonge and Bay streets) with its majestic vaults crossing harmoniously some hundred feet above, the imposing marble water fountain and granite paving stones and the multitude of stairs, escalators and hiding nooks, combine to create a truly exciting playground.

When the hall holds no more secrets, simply turn to the magazines at Great Canadian News.

With all this, one of us (generally yours truly) always manages to enjoy the quiet pleasure of a hot coffee and a newspaper, while the other takes off on further explorations with the kids.

TIPS (fun for 2 years +)
• Before 5 pm, waits at the door of the restaurant are seldom more than 15 minutes.
• Everyone (kids included) is handed a white card at the entrance. You carry this with you and the server puts a stamp on it when you order a dish. This way, the cashier knows what to charge when you exit. You may run a high bill, although the Marché now offers a cheap menu for kids.
• You can access **BCE Place**'s indoor parking lot via Wellington St. It is fairly pricey on weekdays but the weekend flat rate is reasonable.

NEARBY ATTRACTIONS

INFORMATION	Downtown
Restaurant Marché Mövenpick **(416) 366-8986**	**Toronto** **10-min.**

 Schedule: Open daily from 7:30 am to 2 am.
Admission: FREE admission to **BCE Place**. Average cost of a meal is $15-$20/person, kids menu $4 and under.

 Directions: BCE Place at the corner of Yonge and Front Streets, Toronto.

SUMMER SUNDAY CONCERTS

The sound of music

I glance sideways at my little lad, amused by his reaction as music from the 87 ranks and 5000 pipes of the St. James Cathedral's grand organ surrounds us.

Short concerts to broaden children's musical horizon; a lovely church to show them things of beauty grown-ups sometimes create; a cute little garden to stretch their legs; St. James free Summer Sunday concerts are one of those best kept secrets I'm glad to share with you.

With its huge and gorgeous stained glass artwork framing the pulpit, and twelve colourful triptychs adorning the side walls, St. James is a beautiful cathedral of gothic architecture and proportions.

The 30-minute concerts feature a different guest each time, most of whom are organists that perform on the grand organ. The concerts are followed by performances by the **Gentlemen of the Cathedral Choir** ensemble.

While in the area, take a five-minute walk down Church Street southbound then Front Street westbound until you reach the small park by Scott Street, to view the huge trompe-l'oeil mural that adorns the building.

TIPS (fun for 5 years +)

• Don't miss the whimsical store called **Arts on King**, located at 161 King St. East. It is filled with original creations at all prices.
• Down Church St. southbound then east on Front St., you might enjoy the action in the **St. Lawrence Market**; an excellent spot to buy snacks!

NEARBY ATTRACTIONS

INFORMATION	Downtown
St. James Cathedral in Toronto (416) 364-7865 www.stjamescathedral.on.ca	Toronto 15-min.

Schedule: Sundays at 4 pm in July and August.

Admission: FREE
Directions: 65 Church Street (at the corner of King and Church).

CASA LOMA

"I'm the king of the castle..."

Glancing at Casa Loma from the outside is enough to excite young minds. No mistake, we're about to enter a "real" castle.

Don't go expecting the splendor of the European castles (not that the children will care!).

Sir Henry Mill Pellatt, the romantic Toronto financier who had the castle built in 1911, did not enjoy it for more than 10 years before financial problems lead to the selling of the original art and furniture that marked a life of opulence.

Still, the beautiful marbled floor conservatory and the library are testimonies of better times, along with the former apartments of Sir Henry and his wife. What the little adventurers really want to see is the secret staircase hidden behind the wood panelling in Sir Henry's office on the main floor, leading to the apartments. A curving staircase, located on the top floor, leads to the castles two towers, where you can enjoy a great view of the city.

A 250-metre tunnel links the castle with the stables. The tunnel's entrance faces the Gift Shop located on the lower level of the castle. Frankly, this tunnel isn't any more exotic than an unfinished basement. Nevertheless, it intrigues children. Furthermore, it leads to impressive stables. Their mahogany stalls and Spanish tile floors attest to Sir Henry's taste for luxury.

TIPS (fun for 3 years +)

• Hourly parking is available on site. It is often full, but spots are freed rapidly at any hour.
• Next to the gift shop located in the castle's basement, a cafeteria offers an affordable menu with little variety.
• Call to find out about the very entertaining March Break events, Christmas shows and Santa's visit, when the castle is adorned with additional decorations which create a great ambience.

NEARBY ATTRACTIONS

INFORMATION	Downtown
Casa Loma	Toronto
(416) 923-1171	20-min.
www.casaloma.org	

Schedule: Open daily year-round, from 9:30 am to 4 pm (may vary during special events).

Admission: $9/adults, $5.50/ students and seniors, $5/4-13 years, FREE for children 3 years and under.

Directions: 1 Austin Terraces, Toronto. (Take Spadina Street southbound from St. Clair Street West; it becomes Austin Terraces.)

Toronto City Hall in the midst of the action (see page 42).

CULLEN GARDENS & MINIATURE VILLAGE

Tiny, but not trivial...

I found the country cottage of my dreams, only half an hour away from Toronto. It stands at number 77 on a country road in Whitby's Cullen Gardens. It is just perfect: right by a lake, with a shingled roof, adornments of Victorian inspiration and a large veranda. The only problem... it's no more than one metre wide!

What refined precision in the construction of these small buildings (approximately a hundred); all exact replicas of existing buildings you will find outlined in the small plan of the site given at the entrance.

The site includes a number of Toronto landmarks, such as an office building located at 98 Queen Street East, Duncan Farm (Don Mills and York Mills), A. Parrel & Mr. Music stores, a gas station (York Mills and Yonge Street), a stone residence located at the crossing of Highway 401 and Kennedy Road and a dock of blue boats at Queen's Quay.

The small village includes a main road, a residential area, a few estates, a large resort, many secondary residences, a gas station, a church, a fire station and even a campground; all populated with created-to-scale citizens. The postman, the painter, the traveling circus entering the town; the myriad of everyday life details is awesome.

The town's vibrant energy stimulates the imagination. With children playing in the schoolyard, firemen extinguishing a fire (check the real smoke and

smell of burn coming out of the house), paramedics looking for a plane wreck; these little scenarios will enthuse children old enough to recognize them.

There's more to enjoy, with trains and locomotives whistling to announce their arrival on various tracks while children run at their side, yachts sailing, a ferry and many cars travelling the high-

way. Here and there, the familiar sounds of farm animals, sirens, church bells announcing a wedding, planes and even the "woush-woush" of a campground's toilet resonate, adding to the scene's realism.

The "Gardens" of Cullen Gardens appropriately refers to the site's spectacular floral displays, an attraction in its own right, with landscaping enhancing the small residences and their well trimmed bushes. The gardens modify with changing seasons; 80,000 tulips and 300 rhododendron bushes in springtime, 10,000 roses announcing summer, 1,200 mums in the fall. They are adorned with dinosaurs, elephants and other animals sculpted out of the bushes.

There is still a valley with a pond and covered bridge, opening onto a small forest that shades a playground. There, a long suspension bridge will appeal to small children.

You will also find miniature golf, a maze, a large structure to climb and hidden in a barn, a long slide that lands in a haystack.

Close to the snack bar (where you will find affordably priced hot dogs, fries and ice cream), you can cool off at a double wading pool with lovely water slides. You can also catch a pioneer wagon ride.

Around the site, you will find picnic tables, exotic birds in cages and a wishing well. As you leave, take the small path next to the outdoor toilets; it leads to a miniature fairground.

TIPS (fun for 2 years +)

- Don't forget the kids' bathing suits!
- A visit to **Lynde House** is included in your entry fee. The full-scale residence recreates daily life in 1856 and is outfitted with animated mannequins. My son particularly enjoyed the scene depicting two little girls playing "hide-and-seek" in their room and the cat wagging its tail.
- There are fireworks at dusk on Victoria Day and Canada Day weekends.
- Call to find out more about Cullen Gardens' other special events for Halloween and Christmas.
- The outdoor covered snack bar located close to the entrance, is open throughout the year.

NEARBY ATTRACTIONS

Bowmanville Zoo (15-min.)........... p. 26
Jungle Cat World (20-min.)........... p. 28

INFORMATION
Cullen Gardens & Miniature Village
· Whitby
(905) 686-1600
www.cullengardens.com

East of Toronto 35-min.

Admission: $12/adults, $8.99/seniors and students, $5/ 3-12 years, FREE for children 2 years and under, $34.99/ families.

Schedule: Open daily mid-April to beginning of January, from 9 am to 8 pm during the summer and varying hours for the rest of the season.

Directions: 300 Taunton Rd. West, Whitby. Take Hwy 401 eastbound to Whitby, exit Hwy 12, northbound to Taunton Rd. westbound.

DUNDURN CASTLE

Lord of the domain

Outside the 1832 building, a woman in a long dress is plowing the garden. To go inside, we have to walk through an interior courtyard. At the entrance, children play with antique toys to help them remain patient while waiting for the guided tour to begin.

Dundurn Castle is in fact a superb manor that once belonged to one of Ontario's first Premiers, Sir Allan Mac-Nab. The building has preserved much of its initial splendor, with magnificent furniture, trompe-l'oeil walls and original artwork.

In each of the residence's 35 rooms, there's an impressive profusion of vintage objects used in daily life during Victorian times. Among other things, more than one young visitor will wonder where the bathtub is in the children's washroom.

The guided tour, which lasts a bit more than an hour, allows us to admire the manor's three stories. It seemed too long and not interactive enough for my son and he made us leave after 30 minutes. It's too bad, because during the last third of the visit his patience would have been rewarded when visitors get to the castle's underground passages. These stone floor corridors are the only part of the manor that children will readily relate to a "true castle". At the end of the visit, they're expected at the kitchen for a snack of cookies served by employees in period dress.

(Photo : Courtesy of Dundurn Castle/Wordsmith)

The Hamilton Military Museum

The **Hamilton Military Museum** is located on the same site as Dundurn Castle. The Museum visit is included in the Castle admission fee.

Children inevitably stop to look at the large cannon sitting outside the Museum. Small but efficient, this Museum traces military history from the War of 1812 until World War I, using many photos, military uniforms and artillery pieces.

At the entrance, children are given a sheet of paper with pictures of objects they have to find on the site. This treasure hunt is guaranteed to excite them.

Inside the Museum, everyone can ring the alarm bell. In a small, dark corridor, a trench has been reconstructed. The sound effects are very

effective; you will have the uneasy feeling of really being at war!

The **Military Museum** also offers an outdoor Spy Game where kids are given instructions to look all over the historic complex to find five words forming a secret message.

TIPS (fun for 4 years +)
• The Dundurn Castle Gift Shop is well stocked with children's books on castles.
• At Dundurn's restaurant, the atmosphere is a bit too quiet for children. Instead, I recommend that you bring a lunch and eat it on one of the benches found around the Castle.
• Call to find out about their crafts and trades of the 19th century weekend show and their evening in Scotland in August.
• Call to find out about their March Break activities, Fashion Show and Victorian Christmas.

NEARBY ATTRACTIONS
H. Children's Museum (5-min.)..... p. 85
Canadian Warplane Heritage
    Museum (15-min.)................ p. 86

INFORMATION | West of Toronto 60-min.

Dundurn Castle
· Hamilton
(905) 546-2872
Hamilton Military Museum
(905) 546-4974
www.city.hamilton.on.ca/
cultureandrecreation

Schedule: Open daily from Victoria Day to Labour Day from 10 am to 4:30 pm (Military Museum open 11 am to 5 pm); the rest of the year, open Tuesday to Sunday 12 noon to 4 pm (Military Museum open from 1 p.m. to 5 p.m.).

Admission: $7/adults, $6/seniors, $5.50/students, $3/6-14 years, FREE for children 5 years and under, $18/families. Includes access to Hamilton Military Museum.

Directions: Dundurn Park/York Boulevard, Hamilton. Take Q.E.W. toward Hamilton, exit York Boulevard and follow the signs.

CASTLE VILLAGE

Take a peek!

Slightly off the beaten track in the Georgian Bay area, the castle is an intriguing sight in itself. But the little village hidden in its backyard was an even bigger surprise to us when we stopped there on our way back from a great weekend by the beach.

Delightful little houses awaited us, with inviting windows to peek through. Inside, we could see the Teddy Bears' Tea Party, Goldilocks and the Three Bears, Little Red Riding Hood and her grandmother and Mother Goose at reading time. Last year, Snow White and the Seven Dwarfs were added to the collection. All the beautiful small interiors are skillfully decorated with painstaking attention to original detail.

There is also the old mill and dwarf village to climb and slide, the Hansel & Gretel Candy snack bar with tiny tables and chairs, a 222-feet deep well to taste crystal clear water (we were invited to fill our jugs) and a small educational trail.

TIPS (fun for 2 years +)

• The Castle houses a large gift shop and two attractions: a series of small prisons inhabited by a few horror characters ($1) and a section showcasing medieval arms ($2). I was personally much more impressed by the craft involved in the creation of the Enchanted Kingdom.

NEARBY ATTRACTIONS

INFORMATION	Midland
Castle Village Enchanted Kingdom • Midland (705) 526-9683	Region 90-min.

  Schedule: Open Tuesday to Saturday from 10 am to 5:30 pm and Sunday from 12 noon to 5 pm (open Monday in July, August and long weekends). Closed in January, February and March.

Admission: Enchanted Kingdom access is $2/person 2 years and over.
Directions: 701 Balm Beach Road, Midland (Balm Beach Road is north of Highway 12, west of Highway 93).

View from a bastion of the Jesuit mission (see page 117)

❤ Welland Canals Centre

After the gigantic lock gates shut heavily behind a long mastodon, tons of water lifts the ship in ten minutes. It gets even better when sailors working on the decks wave at the children!

(see page 68)

INTRIGUING
MACHINES

Six levels to explore on the Haida (see page 63)

HMCS HAIDA NAVAL MUSEUM

A World War II hero

The Haida, a warship dating back to the Second World War, now rests peacefully and has become a naval museum. For those visitors who weren't born during the war, this heavy artillery ship will wake up the child in them; always seduced by the simplicity and the great noises of war games. However, as entertaining as this attraction can be, we should always keep in mind its historic importance.

In its heyday in 1944, the 377-foot long ship hosted a crew of 250 sailors. During the Korean War, she sailed twice

around the world. The Haida is the last survivor of 27 Tribal destroyers having served in three Commonwealth navies.

More than one young visitor will pretend to attack an imaginary enemy while slipping behind the Haida's cannon and torpedo launchers. Little sailors will be thrilled to criss-cross the destroyer's metallic, bolted depths and its catwalks overhanging the decks. They'll explore all six levels of the ship, enthusiastically climbing ladders and crossing numerous hatchways with great agility.

The more disciplined visitors will guide themselves throughout the ship with the help of a detailed map (given at the entrance), and arrows and numbers.

The engine and the boiler rooms are located down in the hold. On the first bridge, we can see torpedo tubes used to fire torpedoes over the side of the ship. Up high is the bridge from which the ship and the weapons were controlled.

In between, there are the cooks' and stewards' mess, the officers' cabins, the operations room, the radio office, the sickbay and several other rooms vital to the smooth running of a destroyer.

TIPS (fun for 4 years +)

• The Haida's forward guns are fired at exactly 12 noon each day throughout the season, following the sea ports' tradition of signaling high noon to enable sailors to set their chronometers.
• We visited the warship with our baby inside a backpack. The contortions we needed to perform to cross through the numerous hatchways were really uncomfortable for her. Therefore, I don't recommend this visit to parents with young babies.
• On weekends April to June and September until Canadian Thanksgiving, life on the Haida is revived thanks to the Navy cadets who serve on the ship.

NEARBY ATTRACTIONS	
Ontario Place (2-min. walk)	p. 10
The Pier (5-min.)	p. 75

INFORMATION	Downtown
HMCS Haida Naval Museum (416) 314-9755 www3.sympatico/hrc/haida	Toronto 5-min.

Schedule: Open daily, 11 am to 8 pm from mid-June to Labour Day. Open weekends only from Victoria Day to mid-June and after Labour Day until Canadian Thanksgiving.
Admission: $3.95/5-54 years, $2.95/seniors, $9.95/families, FREE for children 4 years and under and for those holding an Ontario Place Play-All-Day pass (see pages 10-11).
Directions: The warship is located east of Ontario Place's entrance.

THE GO TRAIN

One, two, three... GO!

For children fascinated by anything on wheels, the GO Train offers the ultimate experience of a real train journey. Most importantly, it costs a fraction of the price of a regular train ride and you don't end up far from home. Lets not forget it's just as important to enjoy the scenery as it is to know where you're going!

Union Station, on Front Street, is a great starting point for a child's first ride on the GO Train. Suburban and intercity trains are next to one another and children get the chance to see imposing locomotives from up close.

Green and white signs lead us to the GO Train's ticket office and customer service department. When we stopped there to ask for information, they gave my son a few gadgets to celebrate his initiation.

After admiring a large mural decorating the outside of a railcar, we sat on the train's second level to see farther. We were facing south to take in the view of Lake Ontario. Seats are very comfortable and each car is equipped with restrooms... A real train!

After analysing GO destinations, we decided the most interesting was Pickering with the varied panorama of its itinerary: downtown skyscrapers, residential neighbourhoods, countryside and most of all, long stretches alongside Lake Ontario (and in our case, this line passes right in front of our house!). The ride to Pickering lasts 40 minutes and doesn't require a transfer. The train stops at six stations.

To prolong the excursion, you can take the local bus from Pickering Station up to the Pickering Town Centre. We went there to have a bite to eat, play with the toys in the Mastermind Educational shop and throw pennies in the Centre's huge fountain.

TIPS (fun for 3 years +)

• A day pass is sold at the cost of two single fares and allows one person unlimited rides between two specified zones throughout the day of purchase. This is perfect if your young travelers want to get off at different stations and catch the following train.

• To concentrate on the pleasure of the outing, I recommend that you avoid the stress of rush hour, favouring departures between 9:30 am and 2:30 pm. You'll be sure to get a window seat, as there are fewer passengers on board outside peak times! Little ones can be rambunctious without disturbing too much.

NEARBY ATTRACTIONS	
Mövenpick (5-min. walk)	p. 50
Hockey Hall of Fame (5-min. walk)	p. 74

INFORMATION	Dowtown
GO Transit	Toronto
(416) 869-3200	5-min.
www.gotransit.com	

 Schedule: Daily from early in the morning to late at night.

Costs: An adult day Pass for Union-Pickering-Union costs less than $9. It is half the price for children under 12 years and FREE for one child 4 years and under per each accompanying adult.

Directions to Union Station: On Front Street (between Bay and York Streets).

PEARSON INTERNATIONAL AIRPORT

infrequent winds blowing in this direction. Conversely, two east-west runways share the bulk of flights. One of those borders Hwy 401 on the north side. Planes that circulate on it fly just above Hwy 427 and the best way to view them is to reach the Coffee Time restaurant just east of the 427. Real practical isn't it? Between two planes, you can treat the kids to a donut or another snack.

An outing that takes flight

"You're serious? You mean there is not one single viewing window in the entire airport?", I asked baffled. I squeezed my little guy's hand, glancing at him sideways checking for his reaction. Since morning I had been promising him beautiful planes and for the last half-hour had been dragging him around from one end of Pearson airport to the other, in search of an elusive viewing spot.

When I drove my husband to Pearson Airport last year, I realized there is not one single area for viewing the planes in the airport. The disappointingly sad reality prompted me to investigate the issue. Here are the results.

The airport includes a north-south runway that is seldom used because of

The other east-west runway borders Derry Road on the south side and planes that circulate on it fly just above Airport Road. You can view them circulating on the ground from the huge parking lot, owned by McDonnell Douglas, adjacent to the airport.

Judging by the number of cars during our visit, this is a well-known spot for avid observers: couples, tourists equipped with gigantic zoom cameras and children-packed cars.

INFORMATION	West
Pearson Int'l Airport • Mississauga (416) 247-7678	of Toronto 30-min.

 Schedule: Heavy traffic peaks daily between 3 pm and 7 pm, with most impressive sightings on weekends.
Admission: FREE admission to unofficial observation points.
Directions: Coffee Time is located at 215 Carlingview Street, just east of Hwy 427. You reach it via Dixon Road eastbound. The parking lot at McDonnell Douglas is located on Airport Road (a west-end prolongation of Dixon Road). You reach it via Dixon Road westbound.

TIPS (fun for 3 years +)
• You can see planes at closer range from the Coffee Time restaurant. Inside, many window-side tables offer comfortable viewing. With luck, you may be able to park your car in front of the restaurant. If not, there is lots of space in the large parking lot.

NEARBY ATTRACTIONS

SOUTH SIMCOE RAILWAY

Full steam ahead !

Here we are, my son and I, in the middle of nowhere, an hour away from Toronto. Fortunately, the return trip is included. We'll come back to our starting point after a charming, 45-minute ride in a vintage 1920's railcar pulled by a steam engine dating back to 1883.

You have to see the children's eyes when they watch the small train in the distance get closer and finally appear as the colossus it really is, with its whistle and its plume of steam.

Because there's only one track, the locomotive has no other choice but to move forward and then to back up. Mind you, it makes no difference from a passenger's point of view. For part of the ride, we see backyards full of flowers and a few commercial plots of land. Then comes the countryside, with farms, cows, cornfields and trees. Most trees along the track are deciduous and must take on beautiful colours during the fall.

When you're riding, try to make your children listen to what the conductor says. Especially when he is telling the story of the train that disappeared into the river on a foggy night, a long time ago. To put us in the mood, the conductor stops the train and blows the whistle three times, hoping that the ghost of the missing train will answer back…

At the end of the line, we wait a few minutes before heading back. "We're waiting, because all the wheels must be reinstalled for us before we head in the other direction", the conductor seriously explains. It takes kids a few seconds to wrap their minds around that one!

TIPS (fun for 2 years +)

• It's best to get there 20 minutes before departure time. After you've parked and paid for your ticket, you'll be able to wait for the train to arrive (and hear it coming as well).
• Inside the railcars, don't expect luxury. All you need to do is give some of them a good knock to release a 50-year-old cloud of dust! Don't wear white pants...
• There's a small gift shop on the premises which sells, among other things, Thomas The Tank Engine die-cast railcars.
• On hot summer days, you'll be happy to take advantage of the **Tottenham Conservation Area**'s beach and playground, located less than 5 minutes from the train station.
• Call to find out about their Birthday Package, Easter, Canada Day, Halloween and Christmas events and Fall Colour Excursions.

NEARBY ATTRACTIONS

INFORMATION	**North**
South Simcoe Railway	of Toronto
• Tottenham	60-min.
(905) 936-5815	
www.steamtrain.com	

 Schedule: Open Sunday to Wednesday, end of May to end of October, from 10:30 am to 3 pm (10 am to 4 pm on Sundays).
Admission: $10/adults, $9/seniors, $6.50/children 2-15 years, FREE for children under 2 not occupying a seat.
Directions: Take Hwy 400 northbound, exit 55, westbound on Hwy 9. After 15 minutes, turn northbound on Simcoe Road 10. Turn left at the first set of lights after you've entered the town.

STREET CAR MUSEUM

On the right track

We climb into the first vehicle ready to leave. It is a superbly renovated passenger train car from the 1915 – 1960 period. It has elegant woodwork, velvet upholstery and copper tin ceiling decorations. Before long, the car heads towards a lavish green forest.

The Street Car Museum differs from other railway attractions in the region. First, because its primary activity is the collection and renovation of trains, electric tramways and buses. Second, its track system is short (2km). Instead of offering long rides, the museum offers as many short ones as you wish, on any of the different vehicles available that day.

The museum's collection is large, and vehicles are primed for service according to drivers' availability. When we visited, we took a ride aboard the elegant "#8-Steel Car passenger", as well as an open-roof wagon replica of the 1890s,

reminiscent of ancient carriages, in which we enjoyed a ride in nature.

Ten minutes later, our train reached the end of the line at Meadowvale Station, not far from a lovely pond. The kids looked at some old abandoned railcars (most likely future renovation projects), including a run down, but amusing caboose that entertained children 5 years and older. Young visitors also enjoyed the opportunity to walk along the tracks.

An ice cream stand, strategically located by the station and open on the weekends, adds to the outing's pleasure, while washrooms add to its comfort.

Upon your return, you may jump into another train ready to leave, or hang around to admire those displayed in the warehouses or in the yards.

TIPS (fun for 2 years +)

• Make sure to pack some insect repellent; the little bugs are overtly present in the many bushes surrounding Meadowvale Station.
• Call to find out about special events during summer, autumn and Christmas time.

NEARBY ATTRACTIONS
Springridge Farm (20-min.) .... p. 27
Kortright Waterfowl Park (15-min.) p. 29

INFORMATION

West of Toronto 60-min.

Street Car Museum
• Milton
(519) 856-9802
www.hcry.org

Schedule: Opening beginning of May until end of October, from 10 am to 5 pm on weekends & Holidays; and from 10 am to 4 pm on weekdays. (Open weekends only in May, June, September and October; daily in July and August.)
Admission: $7.50/adults, $6.50/seniors, $5.50/3 to 17 years, FREE for children 2 years and under.
Directions: 13629 Guelph Line, Milton. Take Hwy 401, exit 312 (Guelph Line) northbound.

WELLAND CANALS CENTRE

The ups and downs of a canal

A drawbridge lets the freighter go by with its iron ore cargo. The gigantic lock gates shut heavily behind the 225 metre-long ship finishing its course through the canal. Tons of water lift the boat. It gets even better when sailors working on the main deck wave at the children. The kids, confined to the observation platform, look at them with envy. Here in St. Catharines, at Welland Canal's lock number 3, we're swimming amidst a world of Mighty Machines.

The Welland Canal's eight locks allow ships from thirty countries to cross the Niagara escarpment, which brings about a 100-metre level difference between Lakes Ontario and Erie. Because of its ideal set-up for visitors, lock number 3 is the best place to initiate children to the science of locks. It boasts a snack bar, a restaurant, a souvenir shop and the great little St. Catharines Museum. And best of all, the lock's observation platform offers a breathtaking view.

A bulletin board can be found on site, listing the boats that will pass through the lock during the day. It mentions each boat's name, port of registry, length, destination, type of cargo it carries and its approximate time of arrival at the lock. This helps to put young minds to work...

A question of time

During our visit, a good half-hour went by between the moment we saw the arriving freighter passing under the drawbridge and the time it entered the lock. The kids weren't expecting it to be so gigantic!

To help them pass the time while waiting for a ship, we went to the snack bar and explored the playground.

We also visited the St. Catharines Museum. Don't hesitate to go there at any time, as speakers inside the Museum will announce the arrival of each ship. You can then return to the lock and when the ship has finished passing through, resume your visit of the Museum.

It took 15 minutes for the Canadian cargo called the "Jean Parisien" to immobilize itself inside the lock. This allowed us to admire it from every angle. The little sailors accompanying me brought up many questions: "Why is the bridge watered by those hoses?", "Why are there only a few life boats?", etc.

It takes about 10 minutes for the lock to fill with water. The freighter was rising before our very eyes and the kids enjoyed identifying the objects that were getting closer. "Wow, look at the lifebuoy!" "Can you see the white stairs?" "And the blue basket?" Finally, the lock opened on the other side. The freighter's engines restarted and caused the water to swirl around. The ship continued its slow course upstream.

It was about time, as my little sailors' level of interest was beginning to sink dangerously low! We improved the situation by visiting the enjoyable Museum.

The St. Catharines Museum

The highlights of the Museum are the scaled-

down models of the Canal and of a lock and a captain's wheel with a moving landscape seen through portholes in the background.

But unquestionably, the best part of the visit is the **Discovery Centre**, designed especially for children. It includes various activities around the naval theme and several time-travel games.

Among other things, my little inspectors fell in love with the antique phones that really worked and the operator's switchboard, the pioneer children's costumes and the 3-D glasses.

TIPS (fun for 4 years +)

• The lock can remain empty for more than 5 consecutive hours. For a successful visit, it is best to call lock number 3's information service before you leave. It states the daily schedule, with the approximate arrival time of each ship. It is best to go to the site when three or four ships are scheduled to pass through the lock within a 3-hour period.
• The perspective is best when you watch a ship rising from "upbound", that is when it goes upstream from Lake Ontario toward Lake Erie.
• At the Museum entrance, ask for a very interesting booklet called "ABC's of the Seaway". Using simple terms, it describes the functioning of the locks that the kids have just seen live.

NEARBY ATTRACTIONS

Niagara Falls (15-min.).............. p. 104
Wet'n Wild (5-min.)..................... p. 139

INFORMATION	**Niagara**
Welland Canals Centre • St. Catharines 1-800-305-5134 or (905) 984-8880 www.lock3.com	Region 75-min.

 Schedule: Open all year-round from 9 am to 5 pm but ship traffic is interrupted shortly before Christmas and restarts at the beginning of April. Extended hours in July and August. Museum opens from 9 am to 5 pm weekdays and from 11 am to 4 pm on weekends.

Admission: FREE admission to the Centre. Museum admission is $4/adult, $2.50/seniors and students, $2/6-13 years, FREE for children 5 years and under).

Directions: Lock 3, 1932 Government Road, St. Catharines. Take Q.E.W. to St. Catharines, exit at Glendale Ave. West and follow the signs.

♥ Ontario Science Centre

Leaf-cutting ants, 5-metre high tornado, cave, shadow tunnel, space shuttle, bobsled race, soap bubble screen... The Science Centre is indeed a playground offering unlimited resources to those who have the whole world to discover.

(see page 80)

MUSEUMS

CBC Museum & Guided Tours

Behind the scenes

"That's what I like about this job", our guide tells us, "you never know what to expect!" Walking into "the Big Red Box", the Canadian Broadcasting Centre's largest studio, we come face to face with a huge half-constructed pyramid, a modern statue 25 metres high and several walls of look-alike blue ice, all made of styrofoam.

Before entering the 14,000 sq. ft. studio with a high ceiling, you travel through corridors of fake bricks, fake cement and tapestry. We learn the fake bricks are cast from real ones and the paint is peeled off the floors after each production. "How could we make it more real?", asks our guide to the children in our group. "With some birds sounds?" tries a pint-size artistic director.

The tour takes us through the unfinished set of a new soap then out to the studio where the Royal Canadian Air Farce is taped in front of live audiences. We are initiated to the workings of a teleprompter used in reading the news in front of the cameras. From the glassed-in elevator, we admire the Hall's grandiose architecture and the spectacular skylight. We then carry on by ourselves to visit the

CBC Museum's free "Show and Tell" exhibit.

In this quaint space, an area is equipped with microphones and headsets for the benefit of aspiring radio hosts who wish to record themselves telling a story (younger children will likely prefer listening to their parents' recorded storytelling). At the other end of the room, telephones and televisions allow little ones to view and hear excerpts from such productions as The Nutcracker and Cinderella. In a cabin that looks like the inside of a treehouse, kids can view some 20 English or French children's productions; excerpts from CBC/Radio-Canada dating from the fifties.

The back section of the museum is dedicated to puppetry, with the puppets on display also appearing in the excerpts. A lovely puppet theatre, outfitted with viewing monitors to ensure puppeteers are properly hidden from view, sets the stage for improvisation. Not as easy as it looks! Try it!

TIPS (fun for 8 years +)

• The tour is not suitable for younger children but the CBC Museum's free exhibit is entertaining for children aged 3 and up. It is not necessary to pay for the guided tour to access it.
• The guided tour doesn't include a visit to the make-up and props departments.

NEARBY ATTRACTIONS
Playdium Toronto (5-min. walk).....p. 8
CN Tower (1-min. walk)................p. 48

INFORMATION	Downtown Toronto
CBC Guided Tours (416) 205-8605 www.cbc.ca/tours **CBC Museum** (416) 205-5574 www.cbc.ca/museum	

Schedule: Tours schedule vary year-round. You need to call to find out about the month's schedule. The Museum is open Monday to Friday from 9 am to 5 pm, Saturday from 12 noon to 4 pm.
Admission: Tours admission is $7/adults, $5/seniors, students and children 4 years and over (no credit cards). Admission to the Museum is FREE.
Directions: 250 front Street West (across the CN Tower).

ART GALLERY OF ONTARIO

Off the Wall!

The Magic Lantern section in the Off the Wall! room offers a special activity: drawing on a minuscule plastic square. My little artist's jaw drops once his tiny drawing is placed into a slide and changed into a huge and flamboyant mural that appears like magic on the dark wall. That's how AGO turns the newest generation into artists.

This is a great example of what you will find at the Art Gallery of Ontario's (AGO) **Off the Wall!**; quality material, original and intelligent interactive activities and a stimulating environment for your child.

On the weekends during the summer, this hands-on centre located on the museum's lower level is open from 1 pm to 5 pm. As you enter, you can't miss the treehouse that serves as the drawing corner. Behind, a large mural inspired by the Group of Seven welcomes us with the image of a lake and a real canoe.

On the day of our visit, a few families were down on all fours, working hard at an elaborate construction set, inserting a variety of black tubes into one another. Nearby, children played with hundreds of magnetic shapes on a large board; what a contrast to the plastic version we use on the fridge! Once the kids have selected amongst the dozens of costumes and accessories found in the You're Framed section, they get on stage. Behind them, the set is made of a large canvas reproduction of a master's painting. In front of them, their image is projected on a large screen, creating a stun-ning visual. Don't forget your camera!

Finally, there is an industrial quantity of colourful Toobers & Zots foam pieces. It didn't take long before my young adventurer had made himself a helmet and armour with the flexible pieces.

Don't miss **The Grange** next to the Agora restaurant when visiting the AGO's first floor. It is Toronto's oldest remaining brick house and is physically attached to the museum. Children will be handed a sheet with drawings of thirty objects to be found throughout the house.

As a means of introducing children to art, take the kids to the tumblers made out of ostrich eggs and coconuts in room S2! Show them Paul Klee's sketch of his *After the Bath* painting in the small studio of the U14 room and then, have them look for the final masterpiece on the huge red walls.

Take them to see the giant hamburger in room U3. The Contemporary Art section also features a number of really intriguing pieces, even from an adult's point of view.

TIPS (fun for 3 years +)
• The AGO Gift Shop is fabulous and includes many great children's toys. A fancy snack bar is right next to it.
• The AGO is a sure bet for a successful March Break outing! Call to find out about the Family Sundays during fall, winter and spring.

NEARBY ATTRACTIONS
Playdium Toronto (5-min.)............. p. 8
CN Tower (5-min.)....................... p. 48

INFORMATION
Art Gallery of Ontario
(416) 979-6615
or 979-6649
www.ago.net

Downtown Toronto 10-min.

Schedule: Off the Wall! is open Saturday and Sunday from 1 pm to 5 pm. The AGO is open Saturday and Sunday from 10 am to 5:30 pm, Tuesday, Thursday and Friday from 11 am to 6 pm, Wednesday from 11 am to 8:30 pm; it is closed on Mondays. **The Grange** is open from 12 noon to 4 pm (closes at 9 pm on Wednesdays).
Admission: On a "pay-as-you-can" basis ($6 suggested). Does not include admission to temporary exhibits.
Directions: 317 Dundas Street West, Toronto (between McCaul and Beverley).

HOCKEY HALL OF FAME

Shoot and Score!

The Hockey Hall of Fame reflects the colourful palette of the world's many hockey teams and is as bright as any rink during play-offs. There is no need to be a serious fan to enjoy the many attractions displayed throughout the labyrinth-shaped path of discoveries.

The museum fills a large space in the underground of the eye-catching BCE Place. Devoted aficionados could easily spend an entire day reading the texts adjoining each window display (and manipulating CD-ROMs filled with histories, trivia and statistics), but there are also sufficient interactive displays to entertain children 6 years and older, particularly if they are hooked on this national sport.

We enjoyed a large display of goalie masks, from the very first one created by Jacques Plante, to the more recent intricately designed models. Further, a Wayne Gretsky statue breaks through a wall of ice, while a players' locker room recreates minute details (including players' autographed lockers) of behind-the-scenes hockey life.

In one glass room, visitors positioned themselves in front of a goal and tried to intercept pucks that were expelled from a machine. Elsewhere, my son waited anxiously for his turn at "Shootout", where he shot some fifteen pucks toward a board representing a

goalie, which registered data such as his speed, precision and reaction time.

Nearby, a game named "Shutout" provided players an opportunity to see themselves on a screen while intercepting virtual pucks (a daunting challenge for children 8 years and younger).

Another attraction includes small television studios where visitors can transform into sports commentators and watch themselves on the screen. The ability to read from teleprompters enhances the enjoyment of this experience. We sidestepped the challenge by yelling "He scores!".

Make sure to save a few shots to photograph your aspiring players in front of the gleaming Stanley Cup, located in the **Bell Great Hall**. The room is capped by a large dome 15 metres above, adorned with magnificent stained glass. Here, you'll feel the palpable richness of this ex-bank's building. The heavy-door safes are an intriguing sight for children's active imaginations.

TIPS (fun for 6 years +)

• Jerseys from most professional teams are available in small sizes in the boutique you must cross to exit the museum.

NEARBY ATTRACTIONS
Mövenpick (1-min. walk).............. p. 50
GO Train (5-min. walk)................. p. 64

INFORMATION
Hockey Hall of Fame
(416) 360-7765
www.hhof.com

Downtown Toronto 10-min.

Schedule: Open daily year-round, from 9:30 am to 6 pm (opening at 10 am on Sundays) during the summer; opening hours vary around 10 am to 5 pm the rest of the season.

Admission: $12/adults, $7/4-18 years, $32/families, FREE for children 3 years and under.

Directions: Located at the corner of Yonge and Front Streets.

THE PIER WATERFRONT MUSEUM

Ships ahoy!

For 15 minutes, my tiny captain has been having a blast: he's been controlling the water level in the lanes of a miniature lock. Later, he'll pretend to hoist the sails. Then, he'll turn into a pint-size Captain Hook at the costume corner.

We enter the museum through the belly of a hull. Then, we go straight to the telegraph table. We proceed to send some S.O.S. messages. Remember? Three short beeps, three long ones and three short ones? A board detailing the Morse code is displayed to refresh your memory.

In this section of the museum, we peeked through the holes of a frosty glass display case to see the scale model of a shipwreck resting at the bottom of Lake Ontario. We activated the manual air pump linked to a huge antique diving suit.

Six genuine copper boat whistles send kids an irresistible invitation: let's make some noise, lots of it! On the other side, craftsmen are installed in a shop, and work on a boat structure that looks like a dinosaur's rib cage (says my son).

Two rowing ma-chines are placed alongside other memorabilia from Ned Hanlan, Toronto's 1880's world champion sculler. You can start a video-simulated race against athletes. In the back, you will find a spacious discovery centre where children will want to spend the next hour.

A small cushion-lined section is filled with games, books and puzzles. To the left, "steamship" on wheels await kids for a ride around small lighthouses. A variety of costumes allow big and small visitors alike to dress like captains, Edwardian ladies and more. They will pull ropes, tie sailors' knots, play with the lock system and explore Discovery bins.

There's more on the second floor, including: early wooden boats, ship models and a copper bell to ring. Unquestionably, The Pier is designed to interest young visitors.

TIPS (fun for 3 years +)
• Every Monday in July and August, children can make and take an interesting craft. When we were visiting, we built a sailboat out of styrofoam.
• Call to find out about their summer special events, including Canada Day (featuring make-and-take crafts), Halloween weekend and The Pier's birthday packages for children aged 4 to 8.

NEARBY ATTRACTIONS
Toronto Ferry (10-min. walk)......... p. 12
Harbourfront Centre (1-min. walk) p. 38

INFORMATION
Downtown Toronto 5-min.

The Pier, Toronto's Waterfront Museum
(416) 338-7437
www.torontohistory.on.ca/thepier

Schedule: Open daily mid-March to end of October, from 10 am to 6 pm in July and August; closes at 4 pm the rest of the season).

Admission: $5/adults, $4/3-17 years, FREE for children under 3 years.

Directions: 245 Queens Quay West, Toronto (west of Harbourfront Centre, between Rees and Simcoe Streets).

TORONTO POLICE MUSEUM

Good guys, bad guys

Police work is so attractive and conducive to play-acting with its good guys, bad guys and elaborate gear, it will take children twenty years to realize the world of crime isn't cool at all. Until then, the Police Museum makes every effort to impress its visitors.

The architecture of the Police Headquarters building is magnificent. Its museum, worthy of the best, offers plenty of activities which took us an hour to explore.

At the entrance, officers in uniform impressed my little citizen, but not as much as the gleaming police edition Harley-Davidson posted nearby. He happily (and legally!) hopped on the motorcycle. Mannequins display uniforms dating from the 1850's to the present. There's even a Mountie riding a life-size horse.

While your children inspect the genuine police car, read the captions inside the display cases containing exhibits from true criminal cases. After-

wards, initiate your miniature Sherlock Holmes to criminal investigation. You can show them several pieces of evidence: a drinking glass covered with fingerprints, a victim's jewels recovered from the murderer's house and nails stuck in garden hoses used by robbers to slow down the police during a chase.

Adults appreciate watching the short videos covering various topics. We all loved the interactive screen where we tried to draw the portraits of criminals

previously seen in action on a video segment. By touching the screen, we selected the shape of their facial features. The portrait was then compared to the corresponding criminal's face. It was not easy! An interactive fingerprint screen offered another interesting display.

A corridor leads to a prison cell, which is unfortunately closed. Further on, my son saw his first real car wreck. It faces an officer on a 1950's road sign encouraging us to drive safely. The sign compares the number of automobile accident deaths from the current and previous year. The billboard is old, but the statistics are current and updated weekly!

A display of police hats emphasizes the death of several officers. You see, kids, it's not as cool as it looks...

TIPS (fun for 4 years +)

• I suggest that your children watch the video segments about a woman calling 9-1-1 during an emergency. Three screens simultaneously show the woman, the officer on the line and the rescue services set in motion. Impressive and reassuring!
• At the reception, ask for a souvenir police badge!

NEARBY ATTRACTIONS

Mövenpick (10-min.)	p. 50
ROM (10-min.)	p. 78

INFORMATION

Toronto Police Museum
(416) 808-7020
www.torontopolice.on.ca

Downtown Toronto
15-min.

 Schedule: Open year-round from 9 am to 9 pm.
 Admission: FREE (donation)
 Directions: 40 College St., Toronto (one block west of Yonge Street).

CHILDREN'S OWN MUSEUM

A real treat !

My son spontaneously mingled with kids he did not know, and together, they joined in the building of an ambitious dam made of cardboard bricks. When I returned a while later, I found them all walling-in a cooperative dad, whose head barely emerged from the structure.

In fact, the Children's Own Museum (COM) is everything I wish my home could be had I the time, energy, space or money to match my children's creative minds. Consider the **Street Alley** created for kids to draw on walls and floors or the large wall section that changes colour at the touch of warm hands, feet, cheeks and ears (we all know kids' propensity to doodling on walls).

The COM is also a place for hands-on explorations, with the **Art & Junk** workshops for example, where on-going craft activities and collective projects in the making are offered, or the **Cloth Gar-**den with fruits and vegetables to plant and harvest. With the use of wood, fabrics, paper mâché and cardboard, activities at Children's Own Museum offer a refreshing change from today's plastic overuse among toy manufacturers.

The COM is heaven for dress-up aficionados, with its prop room, racks of colourful and glittering clothing, make-up tables and a stage for impromptu performances. Actually, role-playing is high on the COM's priority list with the cutest little nursery, an animal clinic complete with x-ray on the light-board, market place, café, school and post office.

Moreover, there is the **Story Nook:** a space filled with cushions on the floor, books and original artwork by favourite children's illustrators. There is even an **Outside Plaza**, framed by a lovely fence decorated by children, where you might be able to play with earth and water during summer time (I suggest you keep that one for last on your visit!).

TIPS (fun for 2 years +)

• If there's a line-up, you will be assigned a ticket to secure your entrance at a precise time later on (no need to line-up again).
• There is an area on the first floor where you can eat your own lunch, sitting at low tables covered with paper to draw on.

NEARBY ATTRACTIONS

INFORMATION	Downtown
Children's Own Museum	Toronto
(416) 542-1492	20-min.

 Schedule: Open Tuesday to Sunday from 10 am to 5 pm. Closed on Mondays.
Admission: $4.75/person, FREE for children under 1.
Directions: McLaughlin Planetarium Building, 90 Queen's Park, Toronto (south of the Royal Ontario Museum).

ROYAL ONTARIO MUSEUM

computerized re-enactment of a certain species' walk.

The **Bat Cave** is located further on. It is modeled after a true, Jamaican cave. The rocky walls are extremely realistic. You discover the cave's residents when examining its nooks and crannies.

With the help of strobe lights, a swarm of flying bats can be seen (and heard) from time to time. Then, a display of stuffed forest mammals (including a large moose!) will lead you to the great **Hands-On Biodiversity Gallery**.

You'll get their attention

The beauty of a Ming period vase and the mystery of ancient characters leave my son rather cold, as he's not inclined to contemplation. However, the ROM has many ways to get his attention: archaeological digging, discovery boxes filled with surprises, bat cave, dinosaurs, volcano, costumes... Now, you're talking!

For most children, Level 2 is the most interesting floor.

When you arrive at the Museum, go straight to the **Discovery Gallery** on the second floor to ask for tickets giving you access to the site at a precise time. (This way, there's no need to wait in line). If you are with children 4 years and younger, you may want to ask for a timed ticket to the Franklin room in the **Discovery Gallery**.

There will be plenty of other activities on Level 2 to entertain you, until the time on your ticket arrives, starting with the dinosaurs.

Standing on prehistoric flora, embellished with great trompe-l'oeil, the skeletons are quite impressive. "Are they really dead?" asks my son innocently. Indeed! But they can be seen in action at the centre of the room, at the heart of the **Maiasaura Project**. There, young visitors activate a giant screen to see and hear a

Different sections, nicely layed-out with display windows and discovery boxes, give us the impression of being on a field trip in Canada's lake and cottage regions. With guessing games, hands-on tables with skin, fur, bones and horns, beautiful costumes, a tunnel and real beehive, this section is a whole museum in itself.

In the **Discovery Gallery**, equipped with protective glasses, my young paleontologist cheerfully knocked on a wedge with a wooden hammer in order to free a few bones that were set in... cement. Over his head, a tyrannosaurus rex skeleton (a casting more than 5 metres high) oversaw the work.

In the costume room, generously equipped with large mirrors, you can slip on a knight's helmet or a psychedelic outfit from the 1960's. My son was amazed by the weight of the armour he tried.

Parents and children love the large discovery boxes found all over the gallery. Opening each box's cover is the beginning of a new experience. In one of them, you shake a container, then associate the sound produced with the beans and seeds displayed inside the box. In another, you dress figures in period apparel and attempt to identify the appropriate background. In a third one, you try to recognize the scent of spices in their natural state, with the help of their refined version used in our daily lives. There are about twenty such boxes.

You might want to see the mummy in the **Ancient Egypt** section on the third floor before heading back to the main level and the

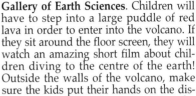

Gallery of Earth Sciences. Children will have to step into a large puddle of red lava in order to enter into the volcano. If they sit around the floor screen, they will watch an amazing short film about children diving to the centre of the earth! Outside the walls of the volcano, make sure the kids put their hands on the display demonstrating the vibrations of an earthquake.

We enter into the other room through an impressive crack made of quartz. There again is an interesting projection room where the image slowly moves from the walls to the ceiling and onto the floor.

Another section leads us through the history of our planet, from the Big Bang to the fossils, with the help of Trog, a rock character as old as the Earth and pretty dismayed by the appearance of bacteria on the planet.

TIPS (fun for 2 years +)

• Bags of all kinds are forbidden inside the **Discovery Gallery**. You may check them, free of charge, at the coat check counter.
• Be careful! The time allotted to each visitor for visiting the Gallery is limited to 30 minutes. It flies by a bit too quickly, especially for kids. To prevent tears, it's better to warn them ahead of time.
• There's a Toronto Parking Authority affordable parking lot on Bedford St., north of Bloor St., one block west of Avenue Road.
• The Museum cafeteria is pleasant and affordable. The Toy Shop located in the basement offers various gadgets, animal figurines and educational books.
• Call to find out about the ROM's March Break activities.

INFORMATION	Downtown
Royal Ontario Museum	Toronto
(416) 586-8000	20-min.
www.rom.on.ca	

Schedule: Open year-round from 10 am to 6 pm Monday to Saturday, 10 am. to 8 pm on Tuesdays, 11 am to 6 pm on Sundays.
Admission: Summer rates are $14/adults, $7/seniors and students, $6/5 to 14 years, $28/family, FREE for children 4 years and under.
Directions: 100 Queen's Park (at the corner of Bloor St. West).

NEARBY ATTRACTIONS
Children Museum (1-min. walk) p. 77
Mt. Pleasant Cemetery (10-min.) p. 92

ONTARIO SCIENCE CENTRE

The science of fun

What a unique playground! Leaf-cutting ants, 5-metre high tornado, cave, CD-ROMs, shadow tunnel, human skeletons, bobsled race, space shuttle; the list goes on. Mind you, nobody has to see it all in just one visit!

In the lengthy corridor by the entrance on Level B, those visiting during the 2000 temporary exhibition, **Timescape,** will be walking along a giant yellow tape measuring the passage of 4.6 billion years. It is completed with over 60 large rock samples from different periods. Look for the one from Sudbury, Ontario, where one of the biggest nickel deposits in the world was formed when a huge volume of the Earth's crust was flash-melted by the impact of a gigantic meteorite, some 1.85 billion years ago.

Timescape, like any temporary exhibit at the Science Centre, is greatly interactive and held in the Great Hall.

I recommend continuing the visit by taking the three escalators down to Level D and starting the tour there with **The Living Earth** to your far right. There is a 5-metre high tornado which moves when you blow on it and a large cave with a TV monitor showing the visitors inside. Up the stairs you can lay on your belly and watch, through a visor, a short movie on a flight from the perspective of the flying bird!

Backing up a bit, in the humid tropical rain forest, don't miss the leaf-cutting ants circulating through transparent pipes.

The activities in the **Communication** room, at the centre of Level D, require a lot of reading so they are more suitable for older children. Everybody, however, will enjoy whispering into the parabolic receptor in order to be heard in the other one at the opposite side of the large room. Some points of interest in the **Technology** room are the Information Highway computers, a giant propeller that a child can turn all by himself and a cyber arm you can manipulate to carry blocks.

Going through the **Transportation** section, go to the level's star attraction, the **Science Arcade**. It has a myriad of sound and visual activities: gyroscopes, electronic keyboards, jiggling sculptures, stroboscopes, steel-drums, a Chinese percussion room and a screen on which you "see" your voice.

When you get in, you are greeted by the "cling clang" of metal balls rolling through intriguing circuits in a series of cause-and-effect reactions. It fascinates the children who may reload the balls themselves.

There is also a circular fabric room that turns around you to create the illusion that you are moving. In another small room, our shadow is projected on to a screen, coloured and processed using special motion effects. A good time to be silly!

Finally, the Arcade is where you will find the famous hair-raising ball used during electrical demonstrations.

Back to the **Technology** room, use the staircase leading to the suspension bridge and Level E. This level houses the **Matter, Energy, Change** section. Young children will either lack the height, strength or patience to obtain the desired results in most experiments. Still, try to make a large screen out of a layer of liquid soap with them and have their shadow printed on the walls of the Shadow Tunnel before heading toward the **Human Body** room.

TIPS (fun for 2 years +)

• Picking up a map of the site at the entrance will allow you to orient yourself better.

• At the Level D entrance, there are several food vending machines and a spacious cafeteria. In the summer, you can go outside and take advantage of the natural surroundings of the ravine where the Centre is located.

• The gift shop on Level A is a fabulous place to buy educational toys, books and gadgets on science. It offers a huge selection of activity books.

• The Omnimax Theatre screen has the shape of a dome, which allows the image to reach as high above and far to the right and the left as your eyes can normally see without moving your head! The 15-minute presentation before the movie is an experience in itself when the children see the apparently solid dome disappear over their heads to reveal 44 speakers. Sound effects will make you think a plane is taking off right in front of you. Visual effects will make kids throw their arms in a Superman fashion to fly through the universe in a tunnel of light.

• You may buy a movie and admission package.

The Natural Defenses module you will find there is quite daring. Ask your little explorers to stand in front of a smiling little girl's picture. Then, open the "window" cut into her face. Behind this opening, her face contracts and a hidden water spray system reproduces a noisy and generous sneeze. It's quite funny when you don't expect it. Just don't tell your kids!

After these mental exercises, kids will be happy to stretch their muscles in the **Sport** room on Level C.

Sportsmen and women can ride sidesaddle, race on a wheelchair and row in place. They can walk on a treadmill while watching their feet in motion on a monitor. Try the bobsled racing simulator. The vehicle vibrates as the bobsled run is flashing by on a monitor right before your eyes.

In the **Exploring Space** section is a favourite: a spaceship cabin containing an instrument panel and four portholes with a view of our moving blue planet. Everything you need to pretend you're being a space shuttle pilot…

Further along, a huge sculpture is displayed near the **Food** room. It represents all the food eaten in one year by an average North American. Children can open dozens of drawers to get a whiff of different spices and smell the air close to the "Push'n Sniff" holes.

And there is more...

NEARBY ATTRACTION

THE BATA SHOE MUSEUM

Little steps in the museum

Since the company has always focused on low-end products, I was quite curious to see what the Bata Shoe Museum had to offer. Well, I was impressed and so was my young companion! The Museum is gorgeous and Bata has shown great skill in putting itself into its young visitors' shoes to get their attention.

The **All About Shoes** exhibition reviews the history of shoes, from prehistoric times until the present, using many props: art reproductions, informative text, mannequins, lighting effects and of course, fascinating artefacts.

The oldest closed shoe dates from the 1400's! You wonder what journey it went through to get here. Among other things, I learned that in 14th Century England, length of the shoe tip was related to social status and regulated by law. That explains the disproportionately long shoes seen in some medieval paintings!

Children can't appreciate the historic value of ancient shoes. But they'll

be impressed by the variety of footwear displayed here, especially if you explain the use of certain shoes to them. This one is for walking on burning sand; that one, to climb glaciers; this other one, to walk on the moon! And what can we say about the ancient Chinese shoes used to reduce the feet of poor women victims of their time? We then move on to the **Star Turns** display, showcasing some famous footwear: one of the Spice Girls platform shoes, one of the Beatles' ankle boots, one of Terry Fox's runners. My little extrovert's favourite was Elton John's massive platform shoes.

Another room is entirely dedicated to dancing shoes from seven periods of ballroom dancing ranging from the 1730's to the 1980's. Above all, the children enjoy the seven Victorian-inspired kinetoscopes, inside of which a turning cylinder activates little characters doing a few dance steps. Unfortunately, it's a bit complicated to raise a child to the height of the opening while turning the cylinder for her... with only two arms.

TIPS (fun for 5 years +)
• Admission is FREE for everyone on the first Tuesday of each month.
• Temporary exhibitions are also offered throughout the year. In the past, we have seen the Raptors' shoes, boots of Siberian nomad tribes, children's shoes and intriguing Japanese footwear.
• Call to find out about March Break activities and children's workshops throughout the year.

NEARBY ATTRACTIONS
Children Museum (15-min. walk) p. 77
ROM (15-min. walk)...................... p. 78

INFORMATION	Downtown
The Bata Shoe Museum	Toronto
(416) 979-7799	20-min.
www.batashoemuseum.ca	

 Schedule: Open Tuesday to Sunday from 10 am to 5 pm. Closed on Mondays and Holidays.

 Admission: $6/adults, $4/seniors, $2/5-14 years, $12/families, FREE for children 4 years and under.

Directions: 327 Bloor St. W., Toronto (at corner of St. George St., west of Avenue Road, and Bloor Street West).

MY JEWISH DISCOVERY PLACE

A museum filled with good faith!

"He'll read all this?" asks my son bewildered as he looks at the series of small papers inserted between the bricks of the "Wailing Wall". I just finished explaining these are children's prayers to God, after they've completed their visit of the museum. On that, he sits down before a blank page and....draws a plane (he'd like to go for a ride). He quickly slips his drawing in a crack in the wall.

Jewish or not, visitors equally enjoy the small interactive museum. In keeping with the Children's Own Museum, for those familiar with it (see page 77), it is a museum dedicated to children between the ages of 1 and 8. It is inspired by a precise theme: the history of the Jewish religion and its current life experience.

Thanks to a series of entertaining and original activities, parents who wish to introduce their children to notions common to all religions, such as compassion, empathy and a desire to do good, can do so with great simplicity.

The section **People Help People** recreates an emergency ward with cardiac intensive care unit. It includes accessories and costumes, complete with various life organs to be reinserted in a dummy's chest. Further, there is an unusual exhibit **You, me and Dignity**, where you can build a miniature playground intended for small handicapped play characters.

At the entrance, the section **Torah Time** recreates a miniature synagogue, with objects for rituals that can be touched, as well as stories that can be re-enacted with felt accessories.

Not too far from the famous **Wailing Wall**, you find a plane structure with a cockpit broadcasting video segments about a trip to Israël. Behind, little kibboutznik apprentices work on an agricultural farm and move large wooden blocks with a small tractor, plant wooden vegetables and pick fabric oranges from an orange tree drawing on a wood panel.

My son transformed himself into a baby elephant from a costume found in a large **Noah's Ark** box. He then proceeded to the top of the ark to join other such animals. Then, he turned on a large spotlight and played with translucent plastic shapes that formed a rainbow on the wall. At the back of the room, he played with a kitchen set to recreate a traditional Sabbath dinner. We ended our visit by making a crown in the crafts section.

TIPS (fun for 1-8 years)

• We interrupted our visit to have a snack at the nearby Second Cup, located in the entrance hall of the community centre that houses the museum. The centre holds a well-stocked kosher cafeteria.

NEARBY ATTRACTIONS	
Black Creek Village (15-min.)	p. 114
Wild Water Kingdom (20-min.)	p. 135

INFORMATION	**North**
My Jewish Discovery Place Children's Museum • North York (416) 636-1880 ext. 456 www.bjc.on.ca	of downtown 30-min.

 Schedule: Monday to Thursday 10 am to 5 pm, Sunday 11 am to 4 pm.

 Admission: $2/person.

 Directions: Bathurst Jewish Centre, 4588 Bathurst Street, North York (north of Sheppard).

MCMICHAEL ART COLLECTION

Inspired hands-on

There is no better way to initiate art appreciation than by taking the kids to a Drop-in Studio activity in the heart of the McMichael museum on a Sunday. Who knows what awaits them? They might create their own sketch book or cut and layer coloured tissue paper into a landscape. When we were visiting, one hands-on workshop was held in the little studio located in front of the museum. Our youngster got to choose from a mountain of socks adorned with glass eyes and rubber noses and made her own animal puppet.

No other painters have better depicted nature than Tom Thompson and the Group of Seven. The Museum holds more than 2000 of their masterpieces.

Seeing Group of Seven reproductions on placemats and stamps has never given me the feeling of being overexposed to their art. Each time, I rediscover them with the eyes of a child. But seeing these paintings with a child is another story, I must admit. An easy way

to do it is to select a theme and have them look for it in the paintings. This treasure hunt may lead to cries of excitement when they spot their theme but... museums are not churches after all!

We criss-crossed all the rooms, looking for autumn leaves on the canvasses. The Museum's walls seemed to my son like storybook pages on which he was looking for coloured trees. Meanwhile, he was noticing that certain landscapes were covered in snow and that people were drawn on others. It became a great observation exercise on the sly.

Wide windows, framing the same nature painters seek to capture, are another reason to appreciate the Museum. Just looking through them makes us want to go outside and play. That's exactly what we did after our tour. A wide path, lined with little trails, undulates through the site.

On our way to the parking lot, we stopped to pet a few bronze wolves resting by the path!

TIPS (fun for 3 years +)

• At the path's entrance by the parking lot, a cafeteria sells a few fresh, affordable dishes. It makes for a perfect transition between a Museum visit and a nature stroll. There's also a restaurant inside the Museum, but its muffled ambience isn't child-friendly.

• Call to find out about great activities for the March Break and Christmas time.

NEARBY ATTRACTION
The S. Simcoe Railway (30-min.) p. 66
The Wave Pool (15-min.)............ p.134

INFORMATION

North of Toronto 45-min.

McMichael Canadian Art Collection
• Kleinburg
(905) 893-1121
www.mcmichael.on.ca

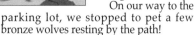

Schedule: Open daily during the summer from 10 am to 5 pm. (The rest of the year, the museum closes at 4 pm Tuesday to Saturday and is closed on Mondays.)
Admission: $7/adults, $5/8-18 years and seniors, $15/families, FREE for 5 years and under.
Directions: Islington Avenue, Kleinburg. Take Hwy 400, north of Hwy 401, exit Major Mackenzie Dr. West, then follow the signs to Kleinburg.

HAMILTON CHILDREN'S MUSEUM

Hamilton for kids

Don't be disappointed by the building's small size. The trademark of the Hamilton Children's Museum is to maximize the use of space. Every aspect of the place's planning and choice of the materials has been well thought out and the results are quite original.

When we first visited, the exhibition topic was: **The city of Hamilton, yesterday and today**. We could play with a huge wooden scale model of the city. There were two superimposed puzzles of a vintage fire truck over a new one, dominos opposing the ancient and modern versions of objects used in everyday life and magnetic boards representing house interiors with movable furniture of the 1840's, 1890's, 1940's and 1990's.

There were also sandboxes from different times for "anthropological" digs, boards explaining different times of the city's history that we had to classify chronologically and so much more.

The last time we visited, a dinosaur exhibit presented several entertaining activities: an archaeological dig, very realistic dinosaur marionettes to perform a puppet show at the Museum's small theatre, a make-your-own dinosaur craft using recycled objects; two computers with dinosaur programs and several dinosaur theme association games and boards. There were even replicas of dinosaur teeth, bones and eggs.

The Museum used to present two different exhibitions every year. Now, it holds a permanent exhibition **In My Neighbourhood** for children 2 to 13 years of age. They intend to improve it regularly. For the time being, it includes role-playing activities related to a construction site, the doctor's office, the police and fire departments and a grocery store.

TIPS (fun for 2 years +)
• A small playground is located beside the Museum. Also, a very large playground can be found 5 minutes away by foot, at the back of the land on which the Museum sits. I didn't see any snack bar in this area. It's best to bring your own picnic.
• The Museum visit doesn't last more than one hour. I strongly recommend combining it with a visit to another attraction in the area.

NEARBY ATTRACTIONS
Dundurn Castle (5-min.).............. p. 56
Canadian Warplane
   Heritage Museum. (15-min.) p. 86

INFORMATION **West** of Toronto 55-min.
Hamilton Children's Museum
• Hamilton
(905) 546-4848
www.cityhamilton.on.ca/
   cultureandrecreation

Schedule: Open Tuesdays to Saturdays, from 10 am to 4 pm and Sundays from 1 pm to 4 pm.

Admission: $2.75/ 2-13 years, one FREE adult with one child, others pay $1.
Directions: 1072 Main St. East, Hamilton.Take the Q.E.W., then Hwy 403 towards Hamilton, exit at Main St. East.

CANADIAN WARPLANE MUSEUM

Down-to-Earth airplanes

When we arrive, children's imaginations are fired up by a real jet, its nose pointing toward the sky like a church steeple. More than twenty genuine, functioning specimens await in the museum's immense hangar. Add cabins, cockpits, switches and buttons to explore and you get a great family outing!

Before entering the hangar, we saw a display on the use of planes in Canadian military history. Budding pilots appreciated watching the illuminated world map and operating the model airplanes. Then, we circulated among the impressive hangar's fleet bathed in natural light. The wheels of certain planes were as tall as my future pilot. Part of the site is dedicated to the restoration of a few vintage models. It's an excellent occasion to appreciate aeronautical engineering while examining airplanes from every angle.

We're not allowed to touch most of the gleaming aircrafts, but don't worry, we can access a few specimens and their engaging cockpits: a real WWII trainer or a real CF-100 jet aircraft. We can also manipulate (from the outside) the array of controls in a Silver T-33 training aircraft. Not often do we get the chance to see a plane's landing gear in action! Children love the two-seat Flying Boxcar simulator, with its wall-to-wall switches and dials.

Stairs at the back of the hangar lead to an observation terrace, from which we have an overview of the Museum's squadron.

Higher up the stairs, we can access the exterior terrace, from which other planes can be seen. At the bottom of the stairs is a vast room with tables, an affordable snack bar and best of all, a panoramic view of the outside. Paved roads connect with the Hamilton International Airport's runways, located 1 km away.

TIPS (fun for 4 years +)
• All aircraft are maintained in flying condition. On most days (weather permitting), you might have the chance to observe a vintage aircraft in flight.
• The Museum gift shop doesn't offer many small gadgets. With loads of model airplanes, it's geared more toward older children. I noticed a children's Top Gun-style test pilot flying suit, sold for approximately $70.

NEARBY ATTRACTIONS
Dundurn Castle (15-min.)................. p. 56
H. Children's Museum (15-min.)..... p. 85

INFORMATION	**West**
Canadian Warplane	**of Toronto**
Heritage Museum	**70-min.**
• Mount Hope	
1-877-347-3359	
or (905) 67-WEFLY	
www.warplane.com	

 Schedule: Open every day 9 am to 5 pm and until 8 pm on Thursdays, closed on Christmas and New Year's.

Admission: $8/person, $7/8-18 years and seniors, FREE for children 7 years and under, $25/families.

Directions: Hamilton International Airport 9280 Airport Road, Mount Hope. Take the Q.E.W. toward Hamilton, then Hwy 403, exit at Fiddlers' Green and follow the museum's signs.

NATURE'S
CALL

HIGH PARK

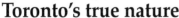

Toronto's true nature

It's all a question of perspective. Previously, I associated High Park with romantic walks along Grenadier Pond and fascinating outdoor theatre with Shakespeare. Now, when I think of High Park, I see a baby bison living in one of Deer Pen Street's many animal paddocks. I hear the little train's bell joyfully ringing through the park's 161 hectares and I see a castle...

There is a trackless little train operating on a seven-station circuit around the park from spring to autumn. You can get on the train at the station of your choice, get off where you want to, and stay as long as you wish before hopping back on. You have the privilege of getting back on at the same station or at the next one, to complete the circuit to your starting point.

The High Park train's flexibility allows visitors to build an itinerary suited to their schedule, to take advantage of the various pleasures offered at the Park.

We prefer to enter the site through High Park Boulevard (accessible from Parkside Road) and turn left to park by the animal paddocks or at the end of Spring Drive. These parking lots are the closest to our favourite spot in the park: the gorgeous **High Park Adventure Playground**.

The playground is next to the big duck pond, the animal pens which house bison, goats, llamas and sheep, a snack bar as well as one of the train's seven stops.

It is simply the most original playground in town. Guess how long it took High Park volunteers to build it from scratch? Ten days! OK, fine, there were about three thousand volunteers and planning had been a long-term affair. Even so, I admire the results of what people can achieve when they put their heart into it.

let small children go there, step up the supervision). When the children have played all they want, I suggest that you let the little train take you to Grenadier Pond, five stations farther (about a fifteen-minute ride for young conductors).

The masterpiece is shaped like a fortified castle, decorated with engravings and mosaics of children's drawings. It occupies 10,000 sq. ft. A third of this area is dedicated to small children and is enclosed with a fence, for parents' peace of mind.

The section for smaller children is full of nooks and crannies to explore and includes an amusing vibraphone. The staircase in the area for older children gives a labyrinth-like impression (if you

In this corner of the Park, the weeping willows that brush against the pond tempt visitors to picnic. Birds are so used to human presence that a Canada goose nearly left a few feathers between the fingers of my little rascal when he was only two years old.

After exploring this area of the Park, you can hop back on the train to come back, ten minutes and two stations later, to your starting point. From there, you can visit Deer Pen Road's twelve animal lodgings.

High Park also includes a large outdoor pool as well as a wading pool, closer to the Bloor Street entrance.

TIPS (fun for 1 year +)

• During the summer months, the Park is not accessible by car on Sundays and Holidays. But don't despair: the High Park subway station (on Bloor St. West) gives direct access to the park's entrance; it is located close to one of the little trackless train stops.

• If you haven't packed any food, you can eat at the **Grenadier Restaurant**, located at the centre of the Park. This very large facility is equipped with a dining room in addition to its enormous cafeteria-style section. The prices are quite decent and the menu is varied: anything from omelettes and pancakes to New-York style steak and souvlakis. It is open year-round from 7 am to 10 pm during the summer (closes earlier the rest of the year) For more information call (416) 769-9870.

INFORMATION	West
City of Toronto (416) 392-8186 www.city.toronto.on.ca	of downtown 15-min.

 Schedule: The Park is open year-round. The trackless train is in operation daily from beginning of May until Labour Day and weekends only in April, September and October.

 Admission: FREE admission to the Park. Train ticket $3/adults, $2/children 2 year and over.

Directions: Located at the intersection of Bloor St. West and Parkside Drive.

NEARBY ATTRACTION
Sunnyside Café (5-min.)............. p. 125

ALLAN GARDENS CONSERVATORY

An oasis in the city

I tell my son we'll be visiting a greenhouse. "Is the house all painted in green?" he asks incredulously. "No, it's a house made out of glass and full of green plants that believe it's summer all year long!" I reply.

Talk about a new greenhouse effect! Five buildings with large windows, covering over 16,000 sq. ft. of plants for all occasions. Some are filled with exhibits which gradually change into new ones according to the plants' life cycles. And it's free!

The first time we visited the hot houses, we were struck by the sweet bouquet and the visual richness of the settings.

Enter through the building with the high dome filled with palm trees. Stepping through a curtain of fine roots, you reach a tropical hothouse with hibiscus set amidst a tapestry-like leafy backdrop. Beyond it, a large selection of hairy, prickly, and fluffy cactuses await the little ones' impatient hands.

Retracing your steps to the other side of the dome, you'll find a cooler space with a small waterfall and a lovely red fish pond with its penny carpeted bottom at the foot of a nymph statuette.

Further, the tropical mood is definitely on with its hot and humid climate. Here, orchids bloom against the roar of water going through a paddle wheel attached to a small house.

TIPS (fun for 2 years +)

• As we finished our visit, we played at guessing from which plant the fallen leaves belonged. A fun initiation to botany!
• There is a small, but free, parking lot you can access from Gerrard Street onto Horticultural Avenue.
• Call to find out about their Victorian Christmas opening ceremony.

NEARBY ATTRACTIONS

INFORMATION	Downtown
The Allan Gardens Conservatory	Toronto 20-min.
(416) 392-7288	
http://collections.ic.sc.ca/gardens	

 Schedule: Open year-round, Monday to Friday 9 am to 4 pm, Saturday, Sunday and Holidays 10 am to 5 pm.

 Admission: FREE
Directions: 14 Horticultural Ave.,Toronto (between Jarvis and Sherbourne Streets, south of Carlton).

GLEN STEWART RAVINE

City trappers

As we happily complete our visit to the Glen Stewart Ravine, my son emerges from our expedition with muddy shoe soles, filthy elbows and knees, soiled pants and a sweater full of twigs, having climbed, slid, splashed about and crawled everywhere. We're perfect candidates for a detergent commercial!

Past the boutiques of Queen Street East in the Beaches and next to Glen Manor Drive, sits a gorgeous rock garden with many water fountains. From there, follow a path to a quaint and leafy park bordering the surrounding mansions.

Walk further, up the stairs and across Glen Manor Drive East, and you find yourself at the mouth of the Glen Stewart Ravine, a paradise worthy of any young Robin Hood! Its "unmanicured" qualities reminded me of the countryside forests of my childhood and won the interest of my aspiring naturalist.

The small and narrow valley in the ravine is crossed by a log-straddled stream a few feet in width. Surrounded by steep tree-filled slopes, some paths and naturally-formed stairs are accessible and comfortably shaded by abundant undergrowth that sits desirably isolated from neighbouring houses.

Walking to the end of the main path bordering the ravine takes about fifteen minutes. Children love to climb the wooden stairs reaching the street, just for the sake of it.

The rugged terrain is not recommended for strollers, and I recommend vigilance with young kids as they can easily slide down (more fright than harm thankfully).

TIPS (fun for 3 years +)
• To avoid exhausting your young travelling companion, I recommend you park on Glen Manor Drive East near the ravine entry. You'll find a place, even on weekends.
• Bring a small plastic or paper made boat and follow its course down the stream. It won't be hard to retrieve when you are finished with the game.
• Warning! If you plan on returning thereafter to civilization on Queen Street, bring a change of clothes for the kids.

NEARBY ATTRACTIONS
Scarborough Bluffs (15-min.)...... p. 95
The Beaches (15-min. walk)....... p. 124

INFORMATION	Downtown
City of Toronto	Toronto
(416) 392-8186	20-min.

Schedule: Open year-round.
Admission: FREE
Directions: Located by Glen Manor Drive East, accessible from Queen Street East.

MOUNT PLEASANT CEMETERY

The circle of life

"Is it true?" asks my anguished son. A smart little girl had just concluded the dispute she had been having with him by striking with an ultimate, irrefutable argument, that had nothing to do with their quarrel: "Oh yeah? Well, girls live longer than boys!" My little live one was shattered when I confirmed this dire statistic. He was ready for a visit to the cemetery to help us approach this delicate but very natural topic in a more realistic fashion.

Few people realize that the Mount Pleasant Cemetery is far from being sinister. The setting is so pretty, it attracts walkers, joggers and cyclists.

Sculptures adorning numerous graves give the visit an interesting cultural quality. If you go to Mount Pleasant Cemetery with children, I suggest you try finding, by car or by foot, the works of art I've photographed for you.

Bayview Avenue and Yonge Street border the Cemetery. It's easier to enter by Yonge Street, north of St. Clair Avenue. Paved roads crisscross the site and cars can stop wherever they please. A tunnel allows vehicles to circulate under Mt. Pleasant Road, which separates the Cemetery into two sections.

After reading for my son a few dates written on gravestones, I was able to discuss with him the random nature of death. Here, parents bid farewell to their child; there, a woman said good-bye to

her husband waiting for the time she'll join him; farther away, an entire family was buried a long time ago.

Many tombstones from plots 37 to 47 even show a picture of the deceased. This confers a more concrete image to the experience. The Cemetery really is a fertile ground for discussion.

NEARBY ATTRACTIONS
Children Museum (10-min.).......... p. 77
Allan Gardens (15-min.)................ p. 90

INFORMATION
Mt. Pleasant Cemetery
(416) 485-9129

North
of downtown
20-min.

Schedule: Open daily, year-round from 8 am to 8 pm.
Admission: FREE
Directions: 375 Mt . Pleasant Rd, Toronto (entrance on Yonge Street, north of St. Clair Avenue).

EDWARDS GARDENS, WILKET CREEK & SERENA GUNDY PARKS

The wheels on the stroller go round and round...

When parents of young children feel the urge for a nature walk, it often means they have to drag wagon and stroller over roots and rocks. So, how about entering a forest of mature, brightly coloured trees, on a fabulous paved trail? How about crisscrossing a singing river that flows underneath several small bridges? You'll find all this in and around Wilket Creek Park, in the heart of Toronto.

OK, fine, I'm only telling you the pretty details. The Don River is polluted and in some areas isn't that crystalline, and several Sunday cyclists and runners rush through the trail. But even so, we really appreciated our invigorating stroll.

I recommend entering **Wilket Creek Park** by the entrance located beside **Edwards Gardens**. The weeping willows, the flowered rock gardens and the

small valleys offer a charming rural panorama, complete with dozens of ducks. Children love to watch them swim in the river. **Wilket Creek**'s wide paved trail takes shape at the end of the gardens.

Along its course, you'll find a few benches, several bridges, smaller beaten dirt paths parallel to the trail, beautiful undergrowth facing the river as well as 30-metre tall maple trees and several other species of deciduous trees that take on magnificent hues in autumn.

You need to walk a good half-hour for the path to cross the road going through **Sunnybrook Park** (where you can find washrooms). We stopped there and retraced our steps.

Those who want to extend their stroll can add the **Serena Gundy Park** trail to their circuit. It's located southwest of Sunnybrook Road, close to the **Wilket Creek** crossing. Moreover, you can park at the entrance of this small park. From there, it takes about ten minutes to reach the end of **Serena Gundy Park**. The exit leads you to Broadway Avenue.

The trees aren't as tall as in **Wilket Creek**, but the trail as a whole is pleasant. Among others, I passed two dog walkers escorted by eight beautiful beasts and a quiet man demonstrating great patience as he was being used as a perch by birds eating out of his hand.

TIPS (fun for 2 years +)
• Another point of interest in the area is accessible by car: in the heart of the **Sunnybrook Park**, you will find an equestrian school. A small stand gives visitors the opportunity to sit while observing horses and riders at work.

NEARBY ATTRACTION
Ontario Science Centre (5-min.).... p. 80

INFORMATION
City of Toronto
• North York
(416) 392-8186
www.city.toronto.on.ca

North
of downtown
20-min.

Schedule: Open year-round.
Admission: FREE
Directions: The Edwards Gardens' entrance is at the corner of Lawrence Ave. and Leslie Street. There are a few pedestrian entrances to Wilket Creek Park on Leslie, south of Lawrence Avenue.

Scarborough Bluffs & Bluffers Parks

No bluffing!

Lying on the fine sand, I'm lulled by the music of waves on Lake Ontario, enjoying the perfect illusion of being by the ocean. We're at the Bluffers Park's beach instead, warmed and cooled all at once by the sun and breeze.

You can reach the base and summit of the stunningly beautiful Scarborough cliffs, some reaching 60 metres high, via Kingston Road. You'll add to your enjoyment of this natural phenomenon if you explore it from top to bottom in one visit.

From above

Take the opportunity of being in the neighbourhood to get a panoramic view of the area, by visiting the **Rosetta McClain Gardens** perched atop the bluffs. You'll catch a breathtaking view of Lake Ontario, 60 metres below.

You can go round the Gardens' paved trails in about twenty minutes.

In the centre, there are symmetrical raised planter beds adorned with a few large stones. A scent garden filled with fragrant plants will titillate little noses. Numerous park benches are set up to allow visitors to admire the landscaping.

Young people like to take refuge underneath a beautiful rotunda located at one end of the Gardens.

I went with my family on a beautiful autumn day. The sun was shining on Lake Ontario and the ground was littered with large leaves in bright yellow and red hues.

On a rainy day, fog created a white screen that completely hid the Lake from our view! The atmosphere was magical. We felt cut off from the rest of the world... but we did not get to see Lake Ontario.

...From below

No need to be hardy to access the bottom of the cliffs. Simply drive back eastbound on Kingston Road, for approximately 5 minutes, and turn onto Brimley Street toward the Lake. The beach spreads at the end of the fourth parking lot to the east. You reach it via a small road that borders the base of the cliffs which sit blazing in the summer light.

This beach, initially quite broad, narrows gradually. When dry, its sand is one of the finest I've seen in the area.

Five minutes from there, you must take the short street west of Midland Avenue to access Midland southbound, until you reach Romana Street westbound; then onto Scarboro Crescent heading south to the **Scarborough Bluffs Park**. As far as I know, this is the only way to access this little park.

Don't be put off by the simple look of the **Scarborough Bluffs Park**, as you can't readily see some fifteen benches sitting at the back. Nothing announces the breathtakingly beautiful panoramic view you'll get from each one. Try them all!

Facing us, the lake spreads endlessly. On the west side, we discover cliffs covered with trees, while the east side reveals the park's 400 acres, with its marina and the cliffs with their rocky peaks. On the park's eastern side, there is a lovely path that borders the cliffs. There, I noticed (just before it heads north), another steeper path going down toward **Bluffers Park**; a natural slide my son really enjoyed.

My little lad threw himself down and made an angel with his arms and legs. Don't forget your beach toys, whatever the season!

As you walk for another ten minutes, you'll discover another source of playful inspiration in the pieces of polished beachwood here and there.

TIPS (fun for 3 years +)

• **The Dogfish Restaurant** at the marina (below Bluffer, the fancy seafood restaurant, and accessible via the second parking lot), serves great hamburgers and fries for approximately $6. Children are admitted, even though it is a pub serving beer. The inside is nondescript, but the outdoor terrace is delightful with a view of the cliffs, the forest and sailboats. It opens at 11 am (**The Dogfish Restaurant**: (416) 264-2338).

• During a visit I made at the beginning of October, I spotted dozens of Monarch butterflies in a patch of wild flowers east of **Scarborough Bluffs Park**. The park is located on their migratory route. I was also intrigued by the multitude of red ladybugs I found every second step on the beach.

• The sight of the cliffs' colourful palette in the October sun is something and the beach that borders them gives a unique feel to the autumn landscape.

NEARBY ATTRACTION
The Beaches (15-min.)............... p. 124

Art on the road

As you stroll along Kingston Road, between Warden and Midland Roads, notice the many murals that adorn certain buildings. It is amusing to ask children accompanying you to spot the ten murals to be found there. See if they can find the race car, ladies in gowns, a row boat and some tubas and drums.

Commissioned by the Scarborough Arts Council, some of the murals are simply superb. I particularly enjoyed the one with a rowboat approaching the cliffs, while my young arts critic was awestruck by the military band.

INFORMATION	East
City of Toronto • Scarborough (416) 338-3278	of downtown 30-min.

Schedule: Open year-round.
Admission: FREE
Directions: Accessible from Kingston Rd. between Midland Avenue and Brimley Rd.

RATTRAY MARSH C. A.

A city's small enclave

Not far from Oakville, you will find a marsh; an unusual site in a residential neighbourhood, it sits sheltered deep within the conservation area.

Rattray Marsh, with its many viewpoints along tree-bordered walkways, attracts young explorers and bird watchers. To reach it, you must first cross **Jack Darling Park**, on the shores of Lake Ontario. The second parking area opens onto a lovely playground. Farther, a tip of land juts out into the lake, surrounded by large stones. We saw a few swans swimming idly by the small beach.

TIPS (fun for 3 years +)

• The long path that borders **Jack Darling Park** is stroller friendly. The boardwalk, however, has too many stairs for comfort. We left our stroller at the entrance to Rattray Marsh.
• The first platform for viewing the Marsh is a little risky, so you should stay close to young children. While the boardwalks are solid, watch the children don't escape to the small slopes. Rubber boots are recommended after a rainfall.
• Locals don't swim in this part of Lake Ontario.
• On weekdays, you can drop in the great indoor playground **L'll Runts & Rascalls** for kids 8-years and under (5-min. drive, 1107 Lorne Park Rd. northbound off Lakeshore Rd. (905) 274-1133).

For those interested in visiting the Marsh, I recommend you leave your vehicle at the third parking area. Anticipate a 20 minute walk through several beaches and another interesting playground, to reach the conservation area.

The path you will cross just before you reach the Marsh, is worth the detour to your left. It opens onto a wide pebble beach.

It will take you a good half-hour to stroll along the boardwalk (excluding frequent stops to satisfy children's curiousity). You may pursue your walk past the Marsh.

As you stroll along this wooden path, make sure to stop from time to time and invite children to listen to and locate the many birds (ornithologists have identified some 277 species on site!). There is a wide range of wildflowers as well.

MOUNT NEMO C. A.

belvedere offers a superb panorama. On a clear day, we can make out the CN Tower, 60 kilometres to the right.

The crevices most accessible to young adventurers are located just left of the belvedere. The two we explored were about 30 metres from the cliff. Their narrow openings slope gently. Five metres down, their bottoms are lined with large stones. Good walking shoes are a must; increased attention is required on certain slippery patches. Natural footbridges cross over the crevices and give access to the edge of the cliff.

Crevices 101

From here, catch the most breathtaking views of the Niagara escarpment. Between the fragrant cedars, you can even admire the Turkey vultures' wingspan while they silently glide at eye level, against a backdrop of checkered fields. Don't worry, there's very little chance that your little ones will fall from this 85-metre cliff without rails. The crevices will prevent this from happening!

Seriously, I was enthralled by the Mount Nemo Conservation Area when I realized that here, children could discover the natural phenomena of cliffs and crevices. During our last visit, we accompanied two mountain climbers, aged four and five, who thoroughly enjoyed these famous crevices.

For little ones on foot or in strollers, there's a wide gravel path (Bruce Side Trail), a shortcut leading to the Brock Harris observation point in 10 minutes. From behind a solid, safe low wall, this

Beyond the first two crevices, the path sometimes gets as close as two metres from the escarpment, and crevices abound. The Bruce Trail is unfit for strollers. Accompanying adults who fear for their children's safety may want to turn back. Others will be rewarded.

Incredibly tortuous, criss-crossed by roots, lined with moss-covered rocks, with spots of light piercing through the trees, this trail is one of the most beautiful I've seen.

The course is clearly marked by white paint on tree trunks. It leads to the parking lot in less than an hour.

TIPS (fun for 4 years +)

• With children 7 years and older, I recommend you take the longest path (the first one to the left when you walk on the gravel path by the parking lot). Kids will love to spot the Bruce Trail's white marks (two marks on a tree means that there's a turn).

NEARBY ATTRACTIONS
Crawford Lake C. A. (10-min.)..... p. 115
Kelso Beach (10-min.)................ p. 133

INFORMATION	**West**
Mount Nemo C. A.	of Toronto
• Mount Nemo	45-min.
(905) 336-1158	
www.hrca.on.ca	

 Schedule: Open year-round.
Admission: $4/vehicle. Deposit the exact amount in an envelope provided at the entrance, or place your same-day entrance receipt to another Halton conservation area on your dashboard.

Directions: Q.E.W., exit at Guelph Line northbound. On Guelph Line, watch for the Colling Road intersection, north of the Mount Nemo village.

BELFOUNTAIN C. A.

Small is beautiful

It's tiny: a 1.5-km trail goes round the Park. However, it's so beautiful! No wonder so many people have their wedding pictures taken here.

It boasts a fountain, a pond, a "cave", a rumbling waterfall and a suspension bridge. The winding path starts up the escarpment and leads us into the depths of the ravine, toward another bridge crossing the crystalline river. Indeed, the Park offers all the elements of a great family outing.

I stumbled upon Belfountain while driving on the beautiful Forks of the Credit Road during the fall. My young wanderer enjoyed this small, tree-lined country road built over several sizeable hills. It leads to Belfountain and to the Belfountain Conservation Area located just before the village.

Bringing a stroller along wasn't a great idea. I had to go down a long series of low steps leading to the river, then continue on rocky trails, while pushing my napping heavyweight angel.

Nice picnic spots lie at the bottom of the steps, by the waterside. Barbecues are available on site. Fishing and swimming were allowed at the time of our visit but the river is fed by springs, so the water is cold!

TIPS (fun for 4 years +)

• To make the most of the stream, bring along rubber shoes or boots.
• After leaving the Park, if you head toward Belfountain, you'll find a snack bar selling ice cream, the perfect grand finale to an outing. The village itself is small, but has a general store that seemed friendly and well stocked.

The original owner, who put up all the other existing structures at the beginning of the last century, built the Park's dike. The fountain is a favourite spot for newlyweds. During our visit, we admired a bride with her elegant wedding party.

The Yellow Stone "mini-cave" is unfortunately closed, but still fires up fertile imaginations. The suspension bridge just downstream from the dam is long enough to impress children.

A stone path begins beside the fountain. It disappears under the trees and runs alongside the roaring river that lies 25 metres below. Now's the time to hold on to your little ones! At times, the path's inclination is quite steep. It eventually leads to a small bridge that stands one metre above a large stream. This area is magnificent during the fall. The kids stopped and played a good while with the stream's running water.

A boardwalk begins on the other side of the small bridge and heads back to the suspension bridge.

INFORMATION | **West** of Toronto 45-min.

Belfountain C. A.
• Belfountain
(519) 927-5838
or 1-800-668-5557
www.mississauganews.com
/conservation/index.html

Schedule: Open Friday, Saturday, Sunday and Holidays 10 am to 5 pm from mid-May to mid-June; open daily 9 am to 8 pm from mid-June to Labour Day weekend; variable hours after Labour Day.
Admission: $3.25/adults, $2.25/3-12 years and seniors, FREE for children 2 years and under, maximum of $14 per vehicle.
Directions: 10 Credit Street, Belfountain. From Hwy 401 westbound, take Hwy 10 northbound, exit at The Forks of the Credit Road, then head westbound.

NEARBY ATTRACTIONS
South Simcoe Railway (20-min.) p. 66
Albion Hills C. A. (15-min.).......... p. 133

ROCKWOOD C. A.

Stunning!

Rockwood Park Conservation Area is a stunningly beautiful place that offers a complete change of scenery, with ruins, caves and natural reservoirs.

I still can't get over it: so much beauty, so close to Toronto and open to everyone. We're lucky…

As you arrive, take the first path on your left after Rockwood's entrance and you will reach large ruins; the site's first attraction.

This old windmill stopped functioning in 1925. It burned down in 1967 and only a few pieces of the stone walls remain today as my aspiring historian discovered. He was captivated by these explanations while he pursued his explorations of the site.

Another road, accessible by stroller, borders the ruins. It leads to two large caves a half-kilometre farther, which I found fascinating. Daylight enters the grottos and children find them amusing to explore. Outside the caves, along the rock walls, make them shout and listen to the echo; it is amazing.

On the other side of the parking lot, you will discover a path that travels around dozens of potholes: some kind of natural tanks of all sizes created by the abrasive whirlpools from glaciers that melted over 15,000 years ago.

While you can't access it with a stroller, it is nevertheless safe and inviting as it turns into small wooden bridges here and there. It borders the Eramosa, a narrow river that runs lazily amidst a fabulous landscape of rock and trees.

Visitors explore it with canoes and pedal boats, which you can rent daily at the beach a little farther inside the park. Rental fee is $10/hour (weekends only, after August). A deposit of $10 is required and life jackets are provided.

With young children, it is preferable to take your car to reach this beach. There, you will also find a small snack bar and washrooms. The beach is really nice with pleasantly smooth sand.

TIPS (fun for 3 years +)
• Bring a flashlight for the children to explore the small cave.
• There's a mini-golf course on the site. It is available at the cost of $4, weather permitting.

NEARBY ATTRACTIONS
Kortright Waterfowl Park (15-min.) p. 29
Street Car Museum (5-min.).......... p. 67

INFORMATION	**West**
Rockwood C. A.	of Toronto
• Rockwood	60-min.
(519) 856-9543	
or (519) 621-2761	

 Schedule: Open beginning of April until mid-October, from 8 am to 9 pm on weekdays and up to 11 pm on weekends.

 Admission: $3.50/adults, $2/6 to 13, FREE for children 5 and under.

Directions: Rockwood Conservation Area, Rockwood. Take Hwy 401 westbound, exit Guelph Line northbound to Hwy 7 eastbound to Falls St.

ELORA GORGE & ELORA QUARRY

Two for one!

At the Elora Gorge, generous rapids attract kayak and tubing amateurs. A few viewpoints from atop the gorge allowed us to observe the courageous athletes practicing their sport twenty metres below.

To gain access to the trails running alongside the gorge, we went down a staircase hidden in a hole through the rock, the discovery of which added to the children's joy.

There's no need to venture very far on either side of the staircase to enjoy the site's beauty. On the trails, roots abound. Near them, trees have grown over large rocks, their roots having had to stretch over one metre to find their nourishment in the earth.

My young hundred-metre dasher is not a natural-born walker. We didn't push the stroller too far on the 8-km circuit that runs through the park. We preferred to drive to **Elora Quarry** while we were still relatively rested. The entrance for one also gives access to the other.

With the passing years, a basin has formed at the bottom of **Elora Quarry**, abandoned since the 1930's. On hot summer days, you can dive into this water fed by pure springs.

We accessed the Quarry through a small beach offering an excellent view of the 12-metre high walls surrounding the body of water. Seen from the beach, the panorama is quite special.

Our little amateur of antiques just loved the manual water pump still in working order located on the beach.

TIPS (fun for 4 years +)
• Close supervision of children is required on the trails at **Elora Gorge**.
• Visitors 42 inches tall and over who want to go down the river on their own tube must buy a $1 wrist band at **Elora Gorge**'s Beach House concession. They must wear a helmet and life jacket. You may rent all of the equipment at the Beach House concession for $18 (with $75 deposit or imprint of credit card).

NEARBY ATTRACTIONS
Kortright Waterfowl Park (15-min.) p. 29
Street Car Museum (20-min.)........ p. 67

INFORMATION	**West**
Elora Gorge & Elora Quarry C. A. • Elora	of Toronto 75-min.

(519) 846-9742 or (519) 621-2761
www.grandriver.on.ca

Schedule: Open May 1st to mid-October from 8 am to 9 pm.
Admission: $3.50/adults, $2/ 6-14 years, FREE for children 5 years and under.
Directions: Take Hwy 401, exit Hwy 6 northbound, turn on to County Rd. 7 to Elora. Turn left at the first light on County Rd. 21. Elora Gorge is on the right. Elora Quarry is located east of Elora.

NIAGARA FALLS

Everybody falls for them

We reached the Falls at noon on a sunny Tuesday. We hadn't missed the long lineups of people waiting to reach Journey Behind the Falls, an attraction at the base of the Falls. The closest parking space was located more than a kilometre away from The Falls! Looking at our three-month-old baby and her "I'd-rather-run-than-walk" older brother, we decided to observe the watery marvel from our car while heading toward the Gorge Adventure.

A couple of kilometres upstream, along the Niagara Parkway, we observed the large cascades as they roared into the Falls. Going downstream, we reached the point where the view embraced the Canadian and American sides of the 55 metre (180 feet) Falls. Through the car's opened windows, we could hear their thundering sound and even feel a slight mist. We eventually got to a magnificent panoramic viewpoint facing the emerald waters whirling in the narrow gorge.

We stopped at the **Great Gorge Adventure**, near the Whirlpool Bridge. There were no lineups and it turned out to be an ideal attraction for young children and quite fascinating for us all. We descended inside an elevator, walked along dark and cool corridors and reached a boardwalk stretching along spectacular rapids.

The river is 38 metres (125 feet) deep at this level, and it makes the water gush down in large impressive swirls at the speed of nearly 64 kph. The fifteen minute walk was beautiful, safe and refreshing (without soaking us).

Back to the car, we continued on the Niagara Parkway, following the river until we arrived at **Niagara Parks Butterfly Conservatory** (see page 32).

There are, of course, a number of other ways to visit the Falls. You can observe them from any one of the many free viewpoints along the road or through a ten minute ride on the **Spanish Aero Car**, a sort of gondola that crosses the gorge some 1800 feet above the river.

There is also a half-hour tour aboard the **Maid of the Mist**, which cruises right to the base of the Falls. Other options include a helicopter tour, a jet boat ride and even a virtual experience at the **Ride Niagara** attraction located under the Rainbow Bridge.

TIPS (fun for 4 years +)

• Everywhere along the Niagara Parkway, my son was intrigued by the long buses of the **People Movers**, a Niagara Parks Commission initiative. These air-conditioned buses with panoramic windows offer shuttle transportation between the Falls and Queenston Heights Park. Transportation cost includes unlimited, all day access to the **People Movers**' buses at any of the stops along the parkway. The best way to see it all! The transportation pass can be bought at the **People Movers** stations around the Falls.

• Niagara Parks Commission offers the Explorer's Passport Plus, a day pass that is advantageous if you wish to include **Journey Behind The Falls**, **Great Gorge Adventure** and **Spanish Aero Car**, with your **People Movers** transportation package. This Pass can be bought at major attractions and Niagara Parks Information Centres, including the **Table Rock Café** Information Centre.

• The **Table Rock Café** is located right by the Falls and offers affordable lunches and children's menu. The view from the tables by the bay windows is priceless.

• The Falls are illuminated at night year-round. Free fireworks can be seen every Friday and on major Canadian and American Holidays at 10:30 pm from mid-May to the first Friday of September.

• You can book timed tickets up to two hours in advance by calling (905) 371-0254. You may pick them up at the attraction 10 minutes before the due time.

Dry fun

The area is chock-a-block with attractions of all kinds in and around Clifton Hill Centre Street. There's the **Guiness World of Records** and the **Ripley's Believe it or not Museum**. Despite some displays of questionable taste, the two will likely strike children's imaginations, whether it be with "the biggest man in the world" or a sculpture made with one grain of rice. One!

The **Fun House**, located at the foot of Clifton Hill Centre, is a colourful little indoor playground. For those keen on stronger sensations, there is the **Ripley's Moving Theatre**, equipped with seatbelts and handles to grab during the more intense moments in the short action-packed films. There's also wax and horror museums and the arcades at **Skylon Tower** and **Minolta Tower Centre** (offering panoramic views).

INFORMATION	Niagara
The Niagara Parks Commission • Niagara Falls 1-877-642-7275 or (905) 371-0254 www.niagaraparks.com	Region 90-min.

 Attractions schedule: Most of the outdoor attractions are open from the end of April until the end of October, at the very least, from 9 am.

People Movers schedule: From 2nd week of June to Labour Day, daily at least from 9 am to 9 pm. (Variable hours for the rest of the season from May 1st to mid-October.)

Admission: Most of the attractions are $5 to $8/adults and $2.50 to $4/6-12 years. **People Movers** all-day pass is $5/adults, $2.50/6-12 years. Everything is FREE for children 5 years and under.

Directions: Q.E.W. towards Niagara; take the exit for Hwy 420, travel 6 km north of the Falls on Niagara Parkway.

NEARBY ATTRACTIONS	
Butterfly Conservatory (5-min.)	p. 32
Marineland (10-min.)	p. 33

Canoeing on the Wye Marsh (see page 107).

WYE MARSH WILDLIFE CENTRE

Water lily land

How about a canoe excursion amidst water lilies and turtles, paddling through corridors of tall grass and bulrushes? Interested? Then, Wye Marsh may be just what you need!

In July and August, you can reserve a seat on one of the seven-metre long canoes that ride on Wye Marsh's waters. As father and son embarked on this one-hour adventure, I took off for a stroll with my younger one toward the beautiful boardwalk that spans the Marsh.

As we approached the wooden trail, we could hear trumpet sounds blowing high and strong. As we moved closer to the large water hole, we discovered that, yes indeed, the noise came from spectacular white Trumpeter Swans, dozens of them, swimming through the channels. A three-storey high tower afforded us a better view of the colony of birds.

On the boardwalk, we found a sheltered section with long landing nets to explore the Marsh's bed. Quite a hands-on experience!

In two places, the trail turns into a bridge and from there, my happy girl greeted her canoeist dad and big brother as they paddled along underneath us. My preschooler could not contain his excitement when he caught a glimpse of some turtles between the water lilies and rocked the boat in a manner none of the other passengers appreciated!

On our way back, we spent some time at the Visitor Centre. There, we listened to samples of waterfowl calls and watched an interesting documentary on the Great Lakes (if not shown when you visit, you may ask for it specifically). My son fell for the poor canoeist who gets caught in time travel and many transformations of his environment (melting of ice, receding of waters, etc).

TIPS (fun for 3 years +)

• Six years is the required minimum age for canoe trips with an adult. Canoe trips depart daily at 10:30 am, 1:30 and 4:30 pm from Wye Marsh. More depart from Sainte-Marie (see page 117) at 12 noon and 3 pm . Kayak trips are also available with an age requirement of 12 years and over. Both need reservations.
• Call to find out about Wye Marsh March Break and Summer Day camps or Parent & Tots programs. Also ask about their great Wye Marsh Festival in September. It is the most active weekend of the year at Wye Marsh.

NEARBY ATTRACTIONS

Castle Village (10-min.).............. p. 58
Sainte-Marie (1-min.).................. p. 117

INFORMATION	Midland
Wye Marsh Wildlife Centre • Midland (705) 526-7809 www.wyemarsh.com	Region 90-min.

Schedule: Open year-round, from 10 am to 4 pm. Closes at 6 pm from July 1st to beginning of September.

Admission: $5.50/adults, $5/4-12 years and seniors, FREE for children 3 years and under. (Canoe ride add. $5/person, kayak ride add. $6)

Directions: Same entrance as Sainte-Marie among the Hurons, Midland. Take Hwy 400, exit 12 West, Wye Marsh is just east of Midland.

❤ Crawford Lake Conservation Area

Children will walk into the fortified village through a corridor lined with 5-metre high stakes. They will climb on top of the palisade like little warriors inspecting their territory. They will explore two Iroquois longhouses and then stroll in the surrounding forest to a boardwalk around the lake. A great way to travel 500 years back in time.

(see page 115)

TIME
TRAVEL

HISTORIC FORT YORK

Kids hold the fort

I'm looking for my son in the crowd walking toward the Fort York entrance. Then I see him lying at my feet. He's immobile, "dead" on the battlefield, a wooden rifle at his side and a smile on his face. I must say that we have just witnessed the re-enactment of the Battle of York, featuring hundreds of costumed actors, real gunpowder and noisy cannon. This would inspire anyone...!

When they discover the historical and archaeological wealth of this Fort, Torontonians are surprised, as they've been passing by for years without noticing it. Nestled between buildings and highways, Fort York is in fact, one of Toronto's well kept secrets.

On this site, the City of Toronto, initially Fort York, was founded in 1793, following the demise of the French Fort Rouillé around 1750.

The **Fort York Festival** is probably the most intense weekend of the year at Historic Fort York and for year 2000, it is being held on July 1 and 2.

During this festival, you can witness mock battles taking place on the grounds surrounding the Fort. You can also observe the actors in their encampment, inside the walls of Fort York, to find out about military life back then.

There are town criers, blacksmith demonstrations, fife and drum parades,

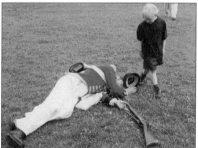

dancing presentations and the most interesting activity for the young crowd: the children's drill.

Little soldiers learn how to hold the wooden rifle, to walk in step, to present arms and to fire at the order of a lenient officer. Giggles are guaranteed; bring out your cameras!

Historic Fort York is open year-round, however, it really comes to life in July and August with its daily demonstrations of musket shooting, music and ironworks, all performed by costumed employees. You're also treated to a historic tasting in the kitchens.

Don't forget the artillery shots that go off punctually every day at noon.

Year-round, you can explore the basement of the Officers' Brick Barracks, built in 1815. More than 12,000 artefacts were found during the archeological digs performed there from 1987 to 1990.

The Blue Barracks house the military museum full of arms and uniforms from different times.

TIPS (fun for 4 years +)

• Special events are particularly interesting for children when they are offering drill sessions. Dates to remember are July 1 and 2 mentioned above and Simcoe Day on August 7.
• When we visited during a re-enactment, children could easily borrow a wooden rifle and bring it along to the battle site.
• Call to find out about their great March Break Time Machine event.

NEARBY ATTRACTIONS

INFORMATION
Historic Fort York
(416) 392-6907
www.torontohistory.on.ca

Downtown Toronto 10-min.

Schedule: In 2000, the Fort York Festival takes place July 1 and 2. Open year-round, Fort York is offering daily activities in July and August from 10 am to 5 pm; shorter hours apply for the rest of the year; extended hours during the March Break.

Admission: $5/adults, $3.25/seniors and students, $3/6 to 12 years, FREE for children 5 years and under. FREE parking.

Directions: At the end of Garrison Road, Toronto. Take Lake Shore Blvd, go north on Strachan Avenue, east on Fleet Street.

MEDIEVAL TIMES

"A thousand years ago..."

"Is that real metal?" asks my son, pointing toward the spear held by the knight greeting us. With just enough authority, the guard scrapes the blade on the stone wall. Gritting our teeth, we conclude that the metal is definitely genuine. "Milady, may I help you?" asks the ticket office attendant, before showing us the way to the table where we will all be crowned.

We find ourselves inside the "castle" antechamber, in front of a camera, alongside a count and countess. We are then pushed gently toward the next activities. During the meal, the $7 photo is presented to us, which we are free to purchase. It did appeal to us, with its medieval-style frame and our hosts' superb costumes!

Inside, the 110,000 sq. ft. space has been turned into a dark, 11th Century castle, complete with coats of arms and murals depicting chivalry scenes. Immediately, the children's attention is caught by a huge, inflated castle inside of which kids bounce like crazy. Young warriors can also launch an attack from a boat and then disembark from it by going down a slide.

There is a fun fight where one attempts to sweep an opponent off his pedestal by swinging a giant "Q-Tip" at him. My 7-year-old just loved it... until he got floored by a menacing older boy. It's not easy being a knight! For $5, you can buy unlimited access to these games.

As we were there early to see the 4 o'clock show, we took advantage of the playroom for half an hour.

To the right of the grand hall, the stables are equipped with windows allowing us to admire the stallions with braided manes. On the other side, royal thrones are surrounded by suits of armour. With great pomp, those who pay an extra fee are knighted during a ceremony.

Around 3:45 pm, the master of ceremonies, to the sound of genuine resounding trumpets, invites us to enter the 1350-seat banquet hall. Wearing yellow crowns, the colour of the knight that we will be rooting for, we head for the tables bearing the same colour.

Over the sand-covered arena, powerful spotlights project an entertaining ballet of coloured lights on a smoke screen. This captivates us until the show begins. We see an act featuring well-trained horses. Then, the handsome, long-haired equestrian warriors are introduced. Guests in each section greet their knight as noisily as possible.

Everyone bursts out laughing when the master of ceremonies describes the people greeting the green knight as "scum" from the bad part of town, invited only thanks to King Alfonso's great generosity. In the cheering department, we cannot manage to outdo the blue section, completely filled by a group of friends, who encourage each other to produce a happy clamour.

The knights confront each other at games of skill, and the queen rewards the best with a flower, which they promptly throw at a beauty sitting in the audience.

At around 4:40 pm, costumed waiters invade the field, armed with chicken-covered trays. "You will love the taste of baby dragon!" our waiter confides to my incredulous son. We will also be offered spareribs, followed by coffee and dessert. The meal is served with soft drinks or water and we eat with our fingers. You will eat to your heart's content, but do not expect a gastronomic feast. (Alcoholic beverages are also available for an additional cost.)

When the knights' performance seems to have ended, the lighting becomes dramatic and a wizard appears amidst the smoke. He warns the court that the Black Knight, son of an enemy

(Photo: Courtesy of Medieval Times)

killed by King Alfonso, is to arrive shortly to avenge his father's death. The king must choose a champion to fight against him.

The knights return to the arena to fight each other in mortal combat (what a waste!) to determine the champion. My son very nearly climbed on his chair to better cheer our yellow knight. "Is he really dead?" inquires my young humanist anxiously when our knight collapses on the floor after a fatal blow. In the darkness, real sparks fly from swords clashing together. I must say that the fights resemble a choreography, which has to be well orchestrated! It is obvious that the well trained actors could easily suffer serious injuries while manipulating the real heavy weapons.

The final confrontation takes place between the champion and the terrifying Black Knight, his red eyes glowing in the dark behind a mask, with Carmina Burana as a musical background.

At 5:45 pm, when we return to the hall, we get down on the dance floor to the beat of non-medieval music! Despite the fact that Medieval Times is an expensive outing (even more so with all the extras that can be purchased), the experience is worth the trip, thanks to dynamic actors and a very entertaining show.

TIPS (fun for 6 years +)
• I recommend avoiding the small dungeon with an exhibit of medieval torture instruments reproductions. Accompanied by graphic drawings, these apparatus bear witness to horrors very difficult to explain to young children. After a fabulous show, visiting this dungeon left a bitter taste in my mouth.
• The gift shop area is chock-full of varied "medieval" goods, from small accessories for children priced at $7 to metal swords going for more than $500.
• You can print a coupon from the Medieval Times website, offering respectively $5 and $3 off on adults and children admission fees (valid Sunday to Friday).

NEARBY ATTRACTIONS

INFORMATION
Medieval Times
(416) 260-1234
www.medievaltimes.com

Downtown Toronto 10-min.

Schedule: Open year-round. Usually Thursdays and Fridays at 7 pm, Saturdays at 7:30 pm and Sundays at 3:30 pm. Call to find out about additional shows or change in schedule.
Admission: $48.95/adults, $31.95/12 years and under. Parking fees vary throughout the year.
Directions: Medieval Times building is located on the west end side of Exhibition Place, Toronto. Take Lake Shore Blvd., go north on Strachan Avenue. The entrance is to your left. There is a parking lot right next to the Medieval Times building.

BLACK CREEK PIONEER VILLAGE

Take a look!

Here, the blacksmith hammers hot red irons; there, a weaver hums as she works. Elsewhere, a homemaker in her long dress bustles about in front of her ovens, while the harness maker handcrafts leather articles. This is Black Creek Pioneer Village: a fascinating replica of a small cluster of some forty houses and businesses of the 1860's.

In fact, Black Creek Pioneer Village satisfies the "voyeur" within each one of us. Here, you can enter anywhere without bothering to knock! (I make sure to point this out to children when we visit). I found it captivating to watch my young explorer open doors by himself and discover new territories.

Many of the rooms inside the houses you'll visit cannot be entered. You may however, view them from the doorway. Thankfully, there is generally an area inside these buildings where you may roam freely and feel as if you were truly in a private house.

If you come with younger children (as I did with my three-year-old son), anticipate their attention span will not exceed 15 seconds for a woodworker silently planing down a plank in the making of a barrel, or a weaver calmly working at her loom.

Other details however, will satisfy their curiosity. For instance, there are farm animals in various parts of the site and after all, the blacksmith makes lots of noise as he hits the red hot iron! We can't forget the treats sold at the old post office!

TIPS (fun for 5 years +)
• Wagon rides are offered during special events.
• Call to find out about Black Creek's fall and Christmas activities (including a visit to Santa) as well as their special Christmas by the Lamplight.

NEARBY ATTRACTIONS
My Jewish Museum (10-min.)..... p. 83
Wild Water Kingdom (15-min.).... p. 135

INFORMATION
Black Creek Pioneer Village
• **North York**
(416) 736-1733
www.trca.on.ca

North of downtown 35-min.

Schedule: Open daily May 1st until December 31st, weekdays from 9:30 am to 4:30 pm, weekends from 10 am to 4:30 pm.

Admission: $9/adults, $7/seniors and students, $5/5-14 years, FREE for children 4 years and under. Parking is $5.

Directions: Located at the corner on Steeles Avenue and Jane Street (east of Hwy 400 and south of Hwy 407). The entrance is east of Jane Street.

CRAWFORD LAKE C. A.

Archaeology 101 at the Indian village

Walking into the fortified village through a corridor lined with 5-metre high stakes is like entering another world. From the top of the palisade, my young warrior inspects his territory with a watchful eye. In such a setting, it's easy to imagine the life of native people who lived here in the 15th Century.

Inside the palisade is the **Crawford Lake Indian Village**, which was reconstructed using data collected during an extensive archaeological dig.

Lifestyle

It is believed that initially, there were five Iroquois longhouses. Unlike traditional teepees, they were shaped like long, windowless hangars and each one housed several families. Two of them have been rebuilt on the site.

The **Turtle Clan House** stands close to the central square. With an austere exterior, it doesn't reveal the exoticism of its interior layout: roof openings to let the rays of sunshine in, fur-covered sleeping areas, animal skins hung here and there, tools, clothing and jewelry.

My little one stuck her nose in the soft beaver pelt and pulled on the raccoon tails, while her big brother examined the forerunners of toboggans, hockey sticks and moccasin slippers, with a puzzled expression on his face. Little cooks could even crush corn at the bottom of a large wooden mortar.

When we visited, a native story-teller was answering questions triggered by this journey back in time.

Inside the second longhouse, the **Wolf House**, a short educational film was shown in a mini-theatre. My little busybody didn't stop to watch the movie, preferring the indoor archaeological site reproduced close by.

He was quite disappointed when he was told visitors couldn't dust the displayed archaeological artefacts.

A third of the **Wolf House** has regained its original look. To help visitors visualize the daily life of the Iroquois of yesteryear, big clan family pictures are hidden behind large pelts. Children enjoy peeking through the holes to discover these worlds.

Where's the lake?

Because of the conservation area's name, we were surprised not to see a lake beside the village. We even hypothesized that **Crawford Lake** didn't exist anymore and that it had been revealed by

TIPS (fun for 4 years +)

• At the counter of the Centre's shop, you can ask for free craft material to make a small object.
• Call to find out about night events, Sweet Water season (March), Earth Day (April), the Indian Summer Festival (September) and Autumn on the Escarpment Celebration (Thanksgiving). During autumn, the colours are magnificent!
• If you present your Crawford admission receipt in other Halton Region conservation areas, you can visit them for free on the same day. Our favourite outing consists of a visit to the **Indian Village** and **Crawford Lake**, going on to Mount Nemo Conservation Area, 10 minutes away by car (see page 99).

NEARBY ATTRACTIONS

excavations. It actually was the other way around: the lake revealed the village!

It is well explained in the pretty Visitors Centre (which abounds in interactive information). The village's presence was discovered after analyzing **Crawford Lake**'s bed. When corn pollen was identified in a sedimentation sample, it became evident that there had been cultivation close by. Research confirmed the hypothesis, and the remains

of the village were then unearthed. A well marked trail leads to **Crawford Lake**. You can go around it by taking a wooden trail, relatively safe for young children. The walk lasts about half an hour. A couple of picnic tables are available by the lake.

Another winding path offers a one-hour return hike into the forest, between roots and crevices, toward a viewpoint on the Niagara escarpment. If you prefer, you can choose to take a safer (and stroller accessible) path with small children. It leads to the belvedere in about fifteen minutes.

INFORMATION
Crawford Lake C. A.
• Milton
(905) 854-0234
www.hrca.on.ca

West of Toronto 45-min.

  Schedule: Open year-round, weekends and Holiday days from 10 am to 4 pm. Open daily May 1st until beginning of September.
Admission: $4/adults; $3.25/seniors, $2.75/ 5 to 14 years, FREE for children 4 years and under.
Directions: Take Hwy 401, exit at Guelph Line South, then follow the signs.

SAINTE-MARIE AMONG THE HURONS

An outing with a mission

Those who received a Catholic education might remember the stories about martyrs in the history books of their youth. Father Brébeuf, the Jesuit mission? Well, it all happened in Midland (close by, actually) in 1649, at Sainte-Marie among the Hurons.

This unique site is a vibrant testimony to the far-reaching impact of European cultural influence and the Christian religion. Judging by the multitude of languages heard during our visit, Europeans know about this and the word-of-mouth mill is going strong!

Before you begin your visit, you may wish to view a 20-minute film to get yourself in the mood. Personally, my little restless companions convinced me to pass and carry on with the rest of the visit. On the other side of the fence, we found costumed attendants busying themselves with chores reminiscent of

the times. A (pretend) Jesuit father was praying in the candlelit chapel; a (real) native storyteller was talking with a few visitors while stirring the contents of a large pot.

Children loved to explore the buildings freely; we adopted their rhythm and therefore did not see everything. Yet, we took time to view the river from above the north-west bastion. The little ones were intrigued by the canoes built in the old tradition.

We climbed up and down the stairs inside the Jesuits' residence, and tried their small beds. Everything here was sculpted in wood, even the plates. We also touched various furs and tried on clothing in the shoemaker's shop. My young trapper was flabbergasted by the small fire an attendant started in the hearth with sparks that flew from two stones he was hitting against one another. Children loved the teepee and three-metre high sunflowers.

At the end of our visit we enjoyed the **Sainte-Marie Museum** and its refreshing coolness. It is decorated with great refinement, even in the texture of its wall coverings. The result of careful and extensive research, the museum harmoniously blends and juxtaposes expressions of 17th Century French culture, the frugal materialism of Canada's early settlers and the native culture.

TIPS (fun for 2 years +)
• Make sure to get a map of the site at the entrance. It will give you an idea of the size of the mission and the twenty buildings to visit.
• Main building includes a cafeteria.
• **Le Festival**, a heritage festival featuring children's activities, costumed re-enactors and more, will be held from July 29 to August 11, 2000.

INFORMATION	Midland
Sainte-Marie among the Hurons • Midland (705) 526-7838 www.saintemarieamongthehurons.on.ca	**Region** 90-min.

 Schedule: Open daily from Victoria Day to Canadian Thanksgiving, from 10 am to 5 pm. Public tours offered early April to Victoria Day and in October.
Admission: $9.75/adults, $6.25/seniors and children, FREE for children 5 years and under.
Directions: Take Hwy 400 northbound, exit onto Hwy 12 westbound. The Mission is located just east of Midland, across the Martyrs Sanctuary.

DISCOVERY HARBOUR

Past and present in the same boat

My son had heard about feathers being used as pens, so he was intrigued by the real one on display in the office of the "Clerk-in-Charge". He could hardly believe his luck when the guide invited him to dip it into the inkwell and write his name in the official register. From then on, my child was hooked for the rest of the excellent guided tour of Discovery Harbour.

In the **Sailor's Barracks**, the guide introduced us to sailors' sleeping habits as she hopped into one of the hammocks that hung one metre over my preschooler's head.

He tried a few times before settling into one. We then played a tossing game the sailors used to play. In the kitchen, separate from the **Commanding Officer's House**, my young cook pretended to mix one pound of this and one pound of that to make a pound cake.

In another barrack, he was absolutely thrilled to sit at a workbench and work with old-fashioned tools, while my youngest one was seriously "re-arranging" the logs in the shed.

Trotting through the **Assistant Surgeon's House**, the **Home of the Clerk-in-Charge**, the **Naval Surveyor's House**; **Keating House** with its long table set for a family, we visited one intimate interior after another and observed a wide range of artefacts from the daily life of the 19th Century.

An afternoon or evening sail is the best way to really enjoy these vessels and the time travel experience they offer. Managed by costumed staff, the cruises are restricted to children aged 10 years and older. Advance bookings are a must.

We explored the vessels' nooks and crannies, tackled the bells, and examined more hammocks in the ship's holds. Meanwhile, my little toddler was busy "reorganizing" the ropes' tight spirals on the bridge...

At the outer limits of Discovery Harbour (a full 30 minute walk from our starting point), we found the site's sole remaining original building: the impressive **Officer's Quarters**, built in the 1840's. The children loved to stroll along its many corridors and climb up and down the stairs. For my part, I was impressed by the collection of period furnishings.

After the tour, we explored two replica schooners, *Bee* and *Tecumseth*, moored at the **King's Wharf**, on our own.

TIPS (fun for 4 years +)

• A special activity program is now offered daily. It includes activities such as model ship making, historic rowing, cannon demonstrations, sailor's ropework, and tea and croquet.
• When muddy, it is hard to push a stroller on the slightly sloped trails; a wagon would be a better option.
• On your way back from Discovery Harbour, you might want to stop at the **Dock Lunch** in the port of Penetanguishene, for tasty fast food and ice-cream at outdoor tables by the water.

NEARBY ATTRACTIONS

INFORMATION Midland

Discovery Harbour   **Region**
• **Penetanguishene**   **90-min.**
(705) 549-8064
www.discoveryharbour.on.ca

 Schedule: Open daily from July 1st to Labour Day, 10 am to 5 pm.
Admission: Selfguided tour is $3.50/person; guided tour is $5.50/person. Special activity program is $3.50 extra per person FREE for 5 years and under.
Directions: Take Hwy 93 north to Penetanguishene, turn right at the water and follow the blue ship logo.

❤ Wild Waterworks

This water park is the perfect size for parents with children of various ages to watch over. The best lazy river, a perfect wave pool, two challenging slides even the small daredevils have access to and an original huge wading pool. Unless you are a teenager, you won't need more!

(see page 137)

WATER GAMES & BEACHES

ONTARIO PLACE

Watch out!

Here, children armed to the teeth, show no mercy and obey no law. Instinctively, they know how to choose their victims in order to derive maximum enjoyment from their hunt. Their favourite target: grownups.

Behind the **Children's Village** awaits the **Waterplay**, designed for children aged 12 and under (measuring less than 60 inches). Think you'll stay dry while accompanying a child to this spray-pad? Think again! A gush from one of the water guns bound to the main fortress nearly yanked my camera from my hands (it was disposable, luckily!).

The **Waterplay** seems like a large miniature golf course, except that the blue of the various small basins full of water replaces the green. The site is well adapted for young children due to its shallow depth. It's also very entertaining for older kids, thanks to its numerous activities. Children cross a suspension bridge, climb on ropes or go from one basin to the other via tunnels (parents

must sprint into the water to pick up their explorer on the other side). Kids also pass under a cascade before throwing themselves into one of two waterslides.

Little ones can hop on a swing in the water, while their older counterparts pump water into water guns by pedaling on a bicycle. They enjoy spraying themselves and their parents! This is the best wading pool I've ever seen.

Older kids will go for more intense water games such as the Rush River Raft Ride, which spans 873 feet (42"+), or the Pink Twister and Purple Pipeline waterslides (both for 42"+), plunging them into the darkness with their enclosed flume. There is also the 50 kph ride through the Hydrofuge (48"+) down a gigantic bowl, ending with a 12 foot drop into the water. I passed on that one!

TIPS (fun for 1 year +)
• Accompanying adults only need ground admission to be with the children. If you wish, a park admission can be upgraded to a Play All Day Pass at many booths throughout the site.
• It's forbidden to eat in the **Waterplay** area. Those exiting the area can get their hand stamped and return after eating.
• More on Ontario Place on page 10.

NEARBY ATTRACTIONS

INFORMATION	Downtown
Ontario Place (416) 314-9900 www.ontarioplace.com	**Toronto** **10-min.**

Schedule: Open daily from Victoria Day to Labour Day (closed during the 4 days following Victoria Day), from 10 am. Closes at 6 pm in May and weekdays in June until mid-June. Closes at midnight the rest of the season.

Admission: Ground admission is $10/6+ years. Play All Day Pass is $24.50/106 cm (42 inches)+ up to 54 years, $11/4 years up to 106 cm (42 inches), $15/55 years+, FREE for children 3 and under (includes the ground admission plus access to all the rides and water games).

Other costs: $9 for parking on the site ($12 to $15 on event days).

Directions: 955 Lake Shore Blvd., Toronto. Located on Toronto's waterfront between Strachan Avenue and Dufferin Street.

HANLAN BEACH

A taste of Paradise

In a glance, we take in the endless stretch of pristine water, with its swimmers frolicking against a backdrop of lazy white sailboats. On the right hand side of the beach, we can watch small

planes taking off from the Toronto Island Airport, outstretched against the city landscape. The CN Tower emerges behind the tree line, reminding us we are still in the heart of Toronto.

The sand is burning our feet on our way to the shore. By the water, it is cooled by the breeze and so soft our kids beg us to bury them in it!

The water is clear and refreshingly cool. It remains shallow for a great distance, reaching no higher than an adult's waist for at least 50 metres. The beach is well patrolled by lifeguards on shore and water.

When we last visited, the beach seemed relatively deserted. Further to our left however, a fenced area with the sign "you are entering a clothing optional area", attracted a larger crowd.

Without being at close range, you see nothing out of the ordinary. Yet, those uncomfortable with the situation can move away along a wide stretch of beach to the right. A small playground and a wading pool mark the entrance to the beach. Beyond the wading pool, a number of smaller sandy trails, some looking like real tiny dunes, branch off from the main trail leading to the beach.

TIPS (fun for all ages)

• A snack bar and washrooms are located near the wading pool.
• From the paved trails beside the wading pool, plan on a twenty minute walk to reach the bicycle rental centre and another ten minutes to reach the Centreville Amusement Park. The little trackless train is not in service anymore.
• More information on Toronto Islands Ferry on page 12.

NEARBY ATTRACTION
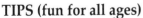

INFORMATION City of Toronto (416) 392-8186	Downtown Toronto Islands

 Schedule: Open year-round.
Admission: FREE, plus cost of ferry ride.
 Directions: Allow for a fifteen minute walk from the ferry at Hanlan Point to reach the small playground. It marks the entry to Hanlan Beach.

THE BEACHES NEIGHBOURHOOD

When you hear the call

Queen Street East, enlivened by small shops, cafés and great parks along the waterfront, indiscriminately attracts three categories of people: those being pulled by their dog, those following their stroller and finally, those who can enjoy a long brunch.

We early risers always begin an outing to the Beaches by having breakfast at one of the district's restaurants in front of **Kew Gardens Park**. We usually head for the **Sunset Grill** and arrive before the 9 am lineup.

We then explore the **Kew Gardens Park** playground. Nestled under tall trees, the playground is equipped with climbing structures for little acrobats.

After playing hide and seek around the "castle" (the rotunda located in the middle of the park), we head for **Kew Beach**, a 3-minute walk away. It's a renewed pleasure each time I look at the water. It sometimes appears turquoise beyond the boardwalk that runs alongside, complete with sand, pebbles and

seagulls. You'd think you were staring at the ocean, as far as your eye can see.

Toward the East, the boardwalk is lined with trees and you cross a few wharves projecting into the lake. The boardwalk ends 20 minutes farther, at **Balmy Beach**. If you walk ten minutes westbound, there's a playground located on the beach as well as the huge Donald D. Summerville outdoor public pool. Beyond, the beach widens a lot and the sand becomes finer. After another 10-minute walk, there's another playground located close to the **Boardwalk Café** and snack bar.

If you walk for another half-hour, you get to **Ashbridge's Bay Park**. You may even park directly in the area surrounding this park (using the Lake Shore entrance, near Coxwell). **Ashbridge's Bay Park** has huge stones where older children love to leap about, tall trees and the softest sand in the neighbourhood.

TIPS (fun for 1 year +)

• Most Torontonians only dare to allow their kids in the Beaches water up to their knees. Read page 123 about Hanlan Beach, the cleanest beach around Toronto.

NEARBY ATTRACTION
Glen Stewart Ravine (15-min. walk) p. 91

INFORMATION	Downtown
City of Toronto (416) 392-1111	Toronto 20-min.

Schedule: Open year-round
Admission: FREE
Directions: The Beaches neighbourhood is located between Coxwell and Victoria Park Avenues, along the waterfront. Take Gardiner Expwy. eastbound, exit Lake Shore Blvd. Turn eastbound on Queen Street East.

SUNNYSIDE PAVILION CAFÉ

Someone pinch me, please!

I'm seated in a café. Facing me, the blues of sky and water merge in an unending horizon. I gaze at two swans flying over the shoreline, hearing the rustle of their majestic white wings. Thirty metres away from me, my son is building a short-lived dam in the fine sand. Beside me, my little one is asleep in her stroller. Sighing with contentment, a flavourful cappuccino in hand, I'm getting ready to relax. Where am I? Here in Toronto, at the Sunnyside Café!

Along Lake Shore Boulevard West, you will notice a large, white building beside a long municipal pool. If you venture to the

other side of this building, you'll discover a façade with arches and columns and a terrace full of tables topped by umbrellas. The structure efficiently muffles the roar of motor vehicles circulating on the adjacent boulevard! Only the boardwalk separates the terrace from the beach.

An inner courtyard boasts other tables set amid fountain, trees and flowers. A beautiful mural completes the illusion of being at a European café, relaxing and writing postcards to friends that have stayed behind.

The restaurant offers an elaborate choice of hearty breakfasts. You can order coffee any way you like it. Salads are large and fresh. Gourmet pizzas are delicious (you will pay around $8 for a fancy burger, $11 for a pizza). The terrace is the perfect spot for adults with children. Parents can finish their meal while watching their little ones play on the beach.

East of the restaurant, beyond the outdoor pool, **Sunnyside Beach** offers a great shaded playground, a large wading pool and a few dinosaurs to climb on! Let's not forget the ice-cream stand by the café.

TIPS (fun for all ages)

• Swimming in the Lake is not recommended but there is a large public pool by the beach and wading pool in the vicinity.
• On rainy days, the restaurant is closed. When the weather is grey, I recommend that you call before you go.
• Free parking is accessible from the Lake Shore Blvd. east of Ellis St. Arriving from the East, take Ellis St. toward the Lake to access the parking lot.

INFORMATION	**West**
Sunnyside Pavilion Café	of downtown
(416) 531-2233	25-min.

Schedule: Open daily April 1st to the end of October, weather permitting, from 8 am to midnight.
Admission: FREE admission to the beach (you pay for what you order).
Directions: 1755 Lake Shore Blvd. West, Toronto. The restaurant is located on the waterfront area below High Park. It stands west of Parkside Drive and east of Ellis Avenue.

NEARBY ATTRACTIONS
Ontario Place (10-min.)................ p. 10
High Park (5-min.)........................ p. 88

CORONATION PARK

Water playground with a view

The water sprays spurting out of the ground and out of posts planted in the pavement wet the children playing on spring-mounted miniature horses and on the seesaw. Facing them, there's a pebble beach with Lake Ontario in the background, as far as the eye can see. No wonder a wise Mom had recommended this Oakville park to me!

I was seduced by the site's set up and by the choice of things to do. The children spent as much time refreshing themselves under the water sprays as they did inventing games with the thousands of plump pebbles.

The large toy truck we brought along worked well. A skipping stones contest kept us busy and I'm still congratulating myself for the pebble I threw that skipped five times.

The spray pad is enclosed inside a fence, and has a lawn and beautiful, tall trees with peculiar knots.

A paved trail leads to the pebble beach located underneath other trees, which allow children to play in the shade. A well-equipped playground is located on the premises. It includes two stimulating structures, one of them wooden with a hanging bridge and a tunnel-shaped slide.

TIPS (fun for 2 years +)

• There is a great indoor playground a five-minute drive away from this park called **Ducky's Play Centre**. Kids 8 years and under will jump, bounce and slide on inflated structures of different shapes (Take Q.E.W. westbound, exit Bronte Rd. South, 549 Bronte Rd., Oakville, (905) 469-1223).

• Call (905) 847-7975 to find out about the Oakville Waterfront Festival in June.

NEARBY ATTRACTIONS

INFORMATION	**West** of Toronto 30-min.
Oakville Parks & Recreation · Oakville (905) 845-6601	

Schedule: Open year-round
Admission: FREE

Directions: Take Q.E.W. westbound, exit at Dorval Drive southbound, turn westbound) on Lakeshore Road.

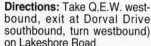

KIDSTOWN WATER PLAYGROUND

A real bargain!

When you accompany a group of young children, you can't expect much more for your money than what you get at Kidstown Water Playground in Scarborough.

This one is like the kid brother of Ontario Place's water park (see page 12). With water spurting bicycles, a water slide that ends in a wading pool, water pistols little rascals will take great pleasure aiming at you from atop the pirate ship and tall water column, this water park will thrill children 8 years old and younger. The older ones will be excited too, if they don't have high expectations from previous visits to larger commercial water parks.

There is also a corridor of spraying rings to navigate, a kiddies' waterfountain and a sandbox. The overall site covers approximately 2000 sq feet and is surrounded by a grassy area with benches and picnic tables. Beyond the fence, there is a colourful playground and a lovely grassy hill down which my little stuntman and his new pals happily rolled.

Kidstown is part of **L'Amoreaux Park South**. A 15-minute walk across McNicoll Ave. will bring you to the large pond of L'Amoreaux Park North where I have frequently seen cranes. Nearby, a small forest and many trails prove nice for family exploration.

TIPS (fun for 1-8 years)

• There are changerooms and the park is entirely framed by a fence. However, the entrance gate is always opened by incoming and outgoing visitors. It is therefore safer to keep a watchful eye on children.

NEARBY ATTRACTIONS

INFORMATION	**East**
Kidstown Water Playground • Scarborough (416) 396-8325	of downtown 35-min.

Schedule: Open daily mid-June to Labour Day, Monday to Friday from 10 am (variable closing times).
Admission: $1/children
Directions: 3159 Birchmount Rd., Scarborough. Take Hwy 401 eastbound, exit Kennedy Rd. northbound, take Finch westbound to Birchmount northbound.

THE AGINCOURT LEISURE POOL

Under the Scarborough palm trees

We often crave turquoise water and palm trees. Then, all things considered, we decide to forget the South for this year. Nevertheless, the Agincourt Recreation Centre pool offers an innovative alternative. It includes aqua-coloured water, waterslides, an adjoining Jacuzzi, a waterside restaurant and... coconut trees as a bonus!

As soon as we went in, the aquatic complex's originality, revealed by wide bay windows, caught my little landlubber's admiring eye and made him walk toward the admission counter, wriggling with impatience.

It wasn't long before my son and other little pirates launched an attack on the fun, shipwreck-shaped waterslide. It is ingeniously sheltered under four towering coconut trees, whose fruit fill up with water before dumping it over our heads.

Behind the wading pool is the small, intermediate pool, perfect for introducing children to swimming. The Recreational Swim program is the only one offered during the summer. It is by far the busiest, as it allows children 7 years and up, measuring 42 inches and more, to swim alone.

During the Recreational Swim, everyone has access to the large, deeper pool. To the right, brave little swimmers are going down the gigantic, spiral-shaped waterslide into a small pool lined with tall palm trees. They are greeted with a loud SPLASH! (Users must measure 48 inches and over.) To the left, adults can soak in the warm waters of the Jacuzzi, also known under the appropriate name of "Conversation Pool". It is heated at 88° F, and is reserved for bathers aged 12 years and up. A bit farther, there's a sauna.

From the pool, there is direct access to the highly rated snack bar, located in a corner of the aquatic complex. Nine tables are especially set up for swimmers in their bathing suits, overlooking palm trees and a view of the pool area. When we visited, the illusion of being down South would have been perfect if observers hadn't been standing on the other side of the bay window, wearing their raincoats.

During the school year, the centre proposes different family programs. I strongly recommend the Parent and Tot program. It is reserved for adults accompanying children 7 years and under, and it isn't crowded.

When we were there, only a dozen children were in the pool along with their accompanying grownup! Only the wading pool and the intermediate pool were open. During Family Swim (another program when every child must be accompanied by an adult), all services are available.

TIPS (fun for all ages)

• Life jackets and beach toys are available for children, don't hesitate to ask for them.

• The Agincourt Centre has a family changing room. You need to bring your own lock if you wish to use the changing room lockers.

• A shop, located close to the admission counter, can help you out if a member of your group needs swimming goggles, a bathing cap, or even a swimsuit, all at a decent price.

• Call to find out about their March Break and Christmas special schedules and their birthday party package.

• Just a few minutes away, east of the Agincourt pool on Sheppard is a very cheap and entertaining indoor playground called **Woodie Wood Chuck's**. It is quite noisy with a section of some sixty token machines. There's a two-floor high climbing structure with three modules connected by tunnels or suspended bridges, hidden corners to explore, ropes, slides, ball rooms, boxing cushions and more. Socks are mandatory. (**Woodie Wood Chuck's** (416) 298-3555, 4466 Sheppard Avenue, Scarborough, $1/person.)

NEARBY ATTRACTIONS

INFORMATION	East
The Agincourt Leisure Pool • Scarborough (416) 396-8343	of downtown 35-min.

Schedule: From beginning of July to beginning of September, Recreational Swim is open Mondays and Wednesdays from 12 noon to 4 pm; Tuesdays from 2:30 pm to 6:30 pm, Thursdays from 1 pm to 4 pm, Fridays 3:30 pm to 8:30 pm, Saturdays and Sundays from 2:30 pm to 5 pm and from 6:30 pm to 8 pm.

Admission: FREE, $2.50/adults coming by themselves.

Directions: 31 Glen Watford Drive, Scarborough. Take Hwy 401 east, exit Kennedy Road, northbound (located north of Sheppard Ave. East, and east of Midland Ave).

BRONTE CREEK PROVINCIAL PARK

Old MacDonald had a pool...

What a gorgeous summer day! Where can you go with children? To the farm? To the pool? There's no need to take a vote. Half an hour away from Toronto, Bronte Creek Park offers a great farm-pool combination, as well as many other sport and leisure activities.

Not only does Bronte Creek Provincial Park have the usual walks and nature centre, it also boasts farmyard animals, a Victorian-style farm where they work the soil in the traditional way and a barn transformed into a most original playground. This park includes a piece of land used as a runway by remote control airplane amateurs. To complete this unique mixture of activities, it offers one of the largest pools in North America.

In this vast park, wanting to try every activity in a single day would be too ambitious. Hardy walkers can move from one attraction to the other by taking the trails and roads laid out on the site. However, young families would be bet-ter advised to travel by car between activity centres, in order to spare everyone's energy.

Spruce Lane Farm

The Bronte Creek visit begins with a walk in the morning (while children are still full of energy!). Coming from the parking lot F, going toward the trails located along Spruce Lane Farm, you have a good chance of seeing one-metre long remote-controlled airplanes doing loops.

The Half Moon Valley trail is an excellent starting point for the whole family. It offers a two-kilometre walk, and is bordered by wildflowers and old trees of unusual shapes.

In certain locations, the wide path runs alongside the wide Bronte Creek as well as the cliff over the ravine in which it flows.

The two storeys of **Spruce Lane Farm**, built in 1899, were laid out in accordance with the times.

During July and August, costumed actors move about, showing visitors a glimpse of the rural life in the early part of the last century. In the kitchen, there's always a little something for us to taste.

Take the plunge

The Bronte Creek Park pool opens at the end of June. It holds 1.3 million gallons of water spread over a 1.8-acre area. An adult must walk 500 steps to go around it! It is fabulous for children: no more than two metres deep in the middle, more than half its area is like a gigantic wading pool where little swimmers can frolic without swallowing mouthfuls of water.

Naturally heated by the sun, the pool's shallow waters are very comfortable during the afternoon. Those who seek shade can plant their umbrellas on the grass around it. Several picnic tables and a snack bar are

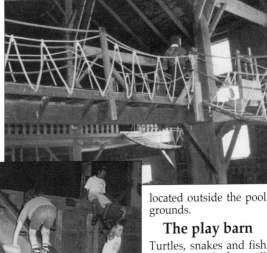

located outside the pool grounds.

The play barn

Turtles, snakes and fish await us inside the small nature centre. There's also a glassed-in beehive, full of activity. The bees go in and out through a long pipe connected to the outside. Not far from there, various buildings house rabbits, hens, chicks, pigs and horses.

All that becomes less interesting when kids spot the great play barn with its hanging bridges, tunnels, large tires to climb on and its second-storey platform from which children can jump on the big cushions, without breaking their necks.

TIPS (fun for 2 years +)

• Bring mosquito repellent if you intend to stroll on the trails. We had some on and really enjoyed ourselves, but I've seen families fleeing from the woods because they weren't protected.
• Call to find out more about Bronte Creek's special events such as Sheep to Shawl on Victoria Day, square dancing, craft & antique shows, Halloween one-day Festival, Christmas Festival of Lights, Maple Syrup Festival and Easter Eggstreme Sunday.

INFORMATION	**West**
Bronte Creek P. P.	**of Toronto**
• Burlington	**35-min.**
(905) 827-6911	
www.ontarioparks.com	

 Schedule: Park opens year-round from 8 am to dusk (play barn, from 9 am to 4 pm). Farm and Nature Centre open daily May 1st to Labour Day from 10 am to 4 pm (weekends only from 11 am to 3 pm the rest of the year). Pool opens daily July 1st until Labour Day from 11 am to 5 pm.
Admission: $4/adults, $3/ seniors, $2/4-17 years, or maximum $12 fee per vehicle. Additional admission fees to the pool: $2.50/adults, $1.50/4-17 years, FREE for 3 years and under.
Directions: 1219 Burloak Dr., Burlington. Take the Q.E.W. westbound to exit 109, take Burloak Drive northbound.

NEARBY ATTRACTIONS
Rattray Marsh C.A. (15-min.)..... p. 98
Coronation Park (5-min.)............ p. 126

PETTICOAT CREEK C. A.

Not a petty pool!

The Petticoat Creek wading pool is huge! It took me over 350 full steps to circumnavigate the edge of this blue wading pool.

There are two of these football-field sized pools located within 30 minutes from downtown Toronto. One is in Bronte Creek Provincial Park (see page 132) and this one is located in Pickering.

The pool is nicely surrounded by green lawn and small trees. We found ourselves a spot in the shade of a conifer tree and we watched our kids run wildly into the shallow water. There's enough water to allow bigger kids to swim in the centre of the pool.

If you think of bringing along some water toys, it will be heaven for children 12 years and under.

Petticoat Creek is located on the shores of Lake Ontario. Outside the fenced pool area are picnic tables and a trail leading to the lakeshore below the

bluffs. The view from above is great, however, don't go expecting a fabulous shore.

TIPS (fun for 2 years +)
• The pool's water isn't heated and remains quite cool in the deeper areas. The sun warms up the shallow section in the afternoons.
• There are changing rooms and a snack bar on the premises
• There are no railings at the edge of the cliff facing Lake Ontario along the trail.

NEARBY ATTRACTIONS
Toronto Zoo (5-min.)..................... p. 19
Cullen Gardens (15-min.).............. p. 54

INFORMATION
Petticoat Creek C. A.
• Pickering
(416) 661-6600

East of Toronto 35-min.

Schedule: Pool is open daily from beginning of June until Labour Day, from 11 am to 7 pm. Park opens at 9 am.
Admission: $9/vehicle to get in the park, $2/person to access the pool.
Directions: Take Hwy 401 eastbound, exit White Rd. South.

Bruce's Mill C. A.

The modest beach in the protected zone of Bruce's Mill borders a reservoir surrounded with bulrushes.

Its narrow stretch sits adjacent to a large grassy area, complete with a small playground. As you go farther around the old factory (hence the name), you can walk to the beginning of a trail system. As you stay on your left, the road eventually forks into several paths, covered by boardwalks in their most spongy areas. There is no snack bar so bring a lunch.

INFORMATION	North
Bruce's Mill C. A.	of Toronto
• Stouffville	30-min
(905) 887-5531	

Directions: Take Hwy 404 North, exit Stouffville Rd. eastbound for 3 km.

Kelso C. A.

To complete a successful outing in the Milton region, I recommend a swim at Kelso Beach.

Of respectable dimensions, the beach sits by a grassy park with lots of shade. It is the ideal spot for a picnic but expect hordes of visitors after 1 pm. The length of the beach is covered with long transparent wires hung some ten metres above, to prevent bird visits. Needless to say the sand is clean! You may wish to hike all the way to the top of the escarpment. It takes more than 30 minutes to reach it from the beach. Kelso is known for its serious trails for mountain bikes. The snack bar is not always open on weekdays; bring a lunch.

INFORMATION	West
Kelso C. A.	of Toronto
• Milton	50-min
(905) 878-5011	

Directions: Take Hwy 401, exit 320 northbound to Campbellville Rd, go westbond to Tremaine Rd., then south.

Heart Lake C. A.

Heart Lake's small beach is spacious. Rented boats criss-cross the heart-shaped pond.

The picnic area bordering the parking lot on the lake's south side, offers an inviting panorama. There, you feel the urge to roll on the grass, but don't count on a view of the lake. Half a kilometre away from the valley's picnic sites, a parking lot borders a lovely little path that rolls up and down for 30 minutes, under the shady coolness of 40-metre high trees. The snack bar is not always open on weekdays; bring a lunch.

INFORMATION	West
Heart Lake C. A.	of Toronto
• Brampton	35-min.
(905) 846-2494	

Directions: Take Hwy 410 northbound until it becomes Heart Lake Road, then go 2 km north of Road #7.

Albion Hills C. A.

Albion Hills' beach is sufficiently long to satisfy those seeking a quiet sandy hide-out.

You can rent a pedal boat or enjoy the small playground that sits near the beach. At the end of the quiet sandy point, you can take a path that borders the lake at its highest point. From there, you can go down a sandy slope that brings you to the shores of the small heart-shaped lake or follow a road along a small river, complete with picnic areas along the way. You must take your car to access other hiking trails of 1.6 to 5.8 kilometre long paths. The snack bar is mainly open during the weekends. You should bring your lunch on weekdays.

INFORMATION	North
Albion Hills C. A.	of Toronto
• Caledon	40-min
(905) 880-0227	

Directions: Take Hwy 400, exit 55; then follow R.R. 9 westbound to Hwy 50 southbound, and follow the signs.

THE WAVE POOL

(Photo : Courtesy of The Wave Pool)

Surf's up!

I had often heard of the Richmond Hill Wave Pool: a huge indoor pool with artificial waves. I was in no hurry to go there with my son. Every time I thought of it, I imagined a heavy swell filled with excited kids who would menace my little tadpole.

How far I was from the truth! Not only is this aquatic complex very secure and exciting for little ones, it's as much fun for older kids.

The spacious Wave Pool aquatic complex forms a harmonious whole, bathed by natural light. Funny fish made of paper mâché decorate the ceiling.

A few tables covered with umbrellas and lined with palm trees are aligned near the bay window. Water sprays and a "rain cloud" hanging from the ceiling wet the swimmers. The centre supplies toys and life jackets.

With the irregular shape, the wave pool looks like a shallow bay you go into gradually, just like at the beach. Over a large 5000 sq. ft. area, the water doesn't go higher than our knees. In this shallow water, the waves are calm, and have the perfect level of turbulence to entertain young children. The big waves sweeping across the rest of the pool and the 160-foot long waterslide are reserved for users able to swim 5 metres independently.

What a surprise! Beside the wave pool is a superb whirlpool delighting young and old alike. It is 70-cm deep and it is kept at a temperature of 96 degrees F.

TIPS (fun for 1 year +)
• Services offered at the pool include a sauna, changing rooms for families and lockers for 25¢ and $1.
• There's no snack bar on the premises. You can eat your own lunch on the glassed-in mezzanine equipped with tables and vending machines. You're also allowed to eat at the tables beside the pool, providing you don't have any glass bottles or containers.
• Call to find out about their March Break and Christmas special schedule and their birthday party package.

NEARBY ATTRACTION
McMichael Canadian
    Art Collection (20-min.).......... p. 84

INFORMATION	**North**
The Wave Pool	of Toronto
• Richmond Hill	40-min.
(905) 508-9283	

Schedule: Open year-round. From July 1st to Labour Day, the Wave swim is open Monday to Friday from 1:30 pm to 4:30 pm, Saturday and Sunday from 1 pm to 4 pm and from 4:30 pm to 7:30 pm. Hours vary throughout the year. Extended hours are offered during Christmas time and the March Break.
Admission: $5.50/16-54 years, $3/3-15 years and seniors, $12.75/families, FREE for children 2 years and under (price for one period, those who want to go swimming twice in the same day need to repay their admission fee).
Directions: 5 Hopkins St., Richmond Hill (southwest of the Yonge/Major Mackenzie intersection). Take Hwy 404 northbound, exit Major Mackenzie Drive West.

WILD WATER KINGDOM

Wild indeed!

Waist-deep in water, hordes of swimmers dance away with the encouragement of a DJ and his music. My 6-year old can't resist the invitation and jumps in (chest-deep), dancing the Macarena with his newfound friends. There is no lack of ambience at Wild Water Kingdom's Caribbean Cove pool!

Wild Water Kingdom, Canada's largest water park, may actually include less slides then the water games section of Canada's Wonderland amusement park, but it is half the price. If you plan to play in the water all day, this is certainly your best bet!

Thirteen body and tube slides, two 7-storey speed slides along with a wave pool, a lazy river and the entertaining pool, are enough to satisfy the legions of teenagers invading the site daily. All slides have a 48-inch minimum height requirement, except the Cork Screw, Side Winder and Little Twister, which are accessible to children from 42 inches in height. Younger children will thoroughly enjoy the large **Dolphin Bay** water playground. It offers beach-like access, small water slides passing through a mushroom, a fish and a frog, a splashing structure with sprays and a tube slide perfect for children 8 years and under, plus wading spots link it all.

Next to the water park are pay-as-you-play activities: a mini golf course, batting cages, bumper boats, volleyball courts and pedal boat rentals for those who want a ride on the reservoir adjacent to the park.

TIPS (fun for 2 years +)

• If you come on your birthday with a valid photo ID, you will receive a free admission to the water park.
• When accompanying children with heights under 48 inches, I recommend Ontario Place or Wild Waterworks (see pages 122 and 137).
• No coolers are allowed on the site (exception is made for parents with babies). We had to take our cooler back to our car.
• You will find on site lockers, snack bars and a shop selling bathing suits.

NEARBY ATTRACTIONS

INFORMATION

West
of Toronto
40-min.

Wild Water Kingdom
• Brampton
(416) 369-9453
www.wildwaterkingdom.com

Schedule: Open from 10 am to 6 pm, weekends only for the first two weeks of June, daily from mid-June to beginning of September, weather permitting (closes at 8 pm July and most August).

Admission: $19.95/10 years and over, $15.50/seniors and under 10 years, $11/after 4 pm. Parking is $6.

Directions: 7855 Finch Ave., Brampton. Take Hwy 427 to Finch Ave. West. Turn westbound and follow the signs.

CANADA'S WONDERLAND

Splash!

Splash Works includes 18 water slides, some of which are 8 storeys tall. They all require a minimum height of 48 inches, except for the Whirl Winds in which adventurers measuring 40 inches or more slide solo on a large tire.

It was not with a light heart that I watched my assertive little boy drag his huge tire for the first time, way up to the launching board of the Whirl Winds. He was so thrilled with his ride that he could not wait to get back in line to do it again! If your child is tall enough and already shows some daredevil inclinations at the local pool, you might want to let her try it too.

All the kids like the Pumphouse located at the heart of **Splash Works**. It features a large coloured structure full of surprising water sprays. It is topped by a gigantic pail that gradually fills up with 3,500 litres of water. Every five minutes, the pail's contents flow forcefully on the heads of delighted children.

The water park also boasts a wide and long Lazy River (36"+) on which an adult and child can float on the same tire and a large wave pool (36"+) equipped with lounge chairs. Children's life jackets are available for free. For the little ones, there's an entertaining wading pool and mini water slides.

TIPS (fun for 3 years +)

• Canada's Wonderland has everything to please children of all ages but for children measuring 40 inches or less, I recommend Ontario Place's huge playground and water games or Centreville's rides (see pages 10, 12 & 122).
• More on Canada's Wonderland on page 14.

NEARBY ATTRACTION
McMichael Canadian Art (15-min.) p. 84

INFORMATION	**North**
Paramount Canada's Wonderland • Vaughan **(905) 832-7000** www.canadaswonderland.com	of Toronto 40-min.

Schedule: Open during the weekends starting the first Sunday in May right through to Thanksgiving weekend and daily from Victoria Day to Labour Day. Open from 10 am to 10 pm minimum (closing times vary).

Admission: (taxes not included) $43/ 7 to 59 years or 48 inches+ tall, $21.50/3 to 6 years and seniors, FREE for children 2 years and under. Grounds Admission only is $23. Parking is $6.50.

Directions: 9580 Jane Street, Vaughan. From Hwy 401, go north on Hwy 400, take exit 33 (Rutherford Road) near Vaughan if you're coming from the South or exit 35 (Major Mackenzie Dr.) if you're coming from the North.

WILD WATERWORKS

Go out with a splash!

From the bounty of water activities offered and the new huge slides accessible to children of all ages, to the immense wave pool, you will find Wild Waterworks leaves nothing to be desired.

You can observe children in all directions from the comfortable green turf by the wave pool which sits in the heart of the action.

The Lazy River (a sinuous water path on which you can flow down atop an inner tube), is the only one I know of that comes equipped with side showers, fountains and nooks and crannies.

My son and his father chose an inflatable double ring to float on and bump me!

The large pool for very young bathers is quite fun with its unusual shape framed by stairs. The water temperature is comfortably lukewarm and doesn't go higher than the knees.

It is full of small fountains that squirt intermittently and little roofs streaming with water.

The two Demon Slides are some six storeys high, much to the delight of swimmers 48 inches tall. I tried them both and found them surprisingly smooth, a little like a gentle toboggan ride.

There are new giant tubeslides offering a 480-foot long drop, with no minimum height requirement.

We visited on a warm but cloudy Saturday afternoon and found the place enjoyably quiet. We never waited more than 5 minutes for a ride on the slides.

TIPS (fun for 2 years +)

• A suggestion for parents with younger non-swimmers wishing to try the large slide. Go down first so that you can assist them when they reach the bottom. There is always a lifeguard on duty.

• There are two snack bars and a restaurant on site. We opted instead for a drive to **Hutch's**. It is a quaint beachfront restaurant at the other end of **Confederation Park**, established in 1940. It serves great "fish'n chips" (the seagulls agreed with me!). There is a colourful playground in the park.

• You have to pay a supplement of $7 ($1 refundable) to rent an inflatable tube to play in the wave pool. The Lazy River tubes included in the admission price remain in the river section.

• General admission drops to $7 if you arrive after 4 pm. This is interesting option if you decide to finish a longer excursion in the area with a dip in the pool.

NEARBY ATTRACTIONS
Welland Canals Centre (20-min.) p. 68
H. Children's Museum (10-min.)   p. 85

INFORMATION	**West**
Wild Waterworks	of Toronto
· Hamilton	50-min.
1-800-555-8775	
www.hamrca.on.ca	

Schedule: Weekends in June and daily from the end of August until Labour Day, open from 10 am to 6 pm. Weekdays in June, open from 11 am to 6 pm. From end of June until end of August, open daily from 10 am to 8 pm. (weather permitting).

Admission: $13.50/adults, $8.50/4 to 10 years and seniors, FREE for children 3 years and under. $7/after 4 pm. Vehicle entrance to Confederation Park is $6.50 (with in and out priviledges).

Directions : Take Q.E.W to the Centennial Parkway (Hwy 20). Travel northbound toward the Lake, follow signs.

WET'N WILD

Happy hour

People seem to vanish from water parks after 4 pm and true to form, this was the case when we stopped at Wet'n Wild on our way back from Niagara Falls. We found no lineups, there was the benefit of lower admission fees and a less hazardous sun under which to enjoy the two hours of play before closing time... Definitely the best way to end the day on a cool note.

Wet'n Wild is not a big water park. It would be better described as a small amusement park with a large water games section. This section consists of a small wave pool, a cute drifter river running around a sandy island (on which you can land), two different water slides and a large wading pool with spray poles.

Unlimited access to bumper boats, bumper cars and "Tilt a whirl" rides that will make you dizzy, are included in the admission fee. Other attractions include: mini-golf (with a $1 deposit), ride on a go-kart ($2) and access to a rock climbing wall ($2).

INFORMATION
Wet'n Wild
• Vineland Station
1-800-263-9453
or (905) 562-7304

Niagara Region 70-min.

Schedule: Open the second weekend of June with variable schedule, then open daily end of June until Labour Day from 10 am to 8 pm (weather permitting).

Admission: $10.95/5 years and over, FREE for children 4 years and under, $4.25/after 4 pm.

Directions: 3293 North Service Road (Prudhomme Blvd), Vineland Station. Take Q.E.W. in direction to Niagara, exit #56 & # 57 (Victoria Ave.) toward the Lake, then go eastbound on North Service Road (Prudhomme Blvd.).

TIPS (fun for 3 years +)
• Picnic tables are located at the adjacent park and some face Lake Ontario. You may use them when the area is not reserved by groups.
• Children must be 42 inches tall and know how to swim to have access to the two water slides. Young children may try the drifter river, if they are escorted by an adult on a tube next to them.
• Children under 12 years may ride the go-karts with an adult driver.

NEARBY ATTRACTIONS
Welland Canals Centre (15-min.) p. 68
Niagara Falls (25-min.)................ p. 104

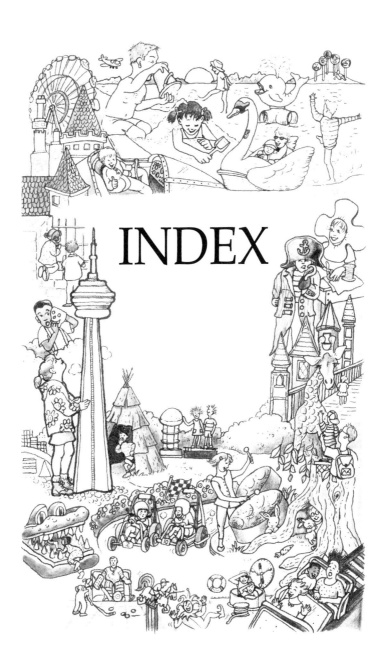

INDEX

ALPHABETICAL INDEX

LOCATION INDEX